What Did th

ALSO BY MARION COUTTS

The Iceberg

What Did the Deep Sea Say?

MARION COUTTS

FERN
PRESS

1 3 5 7 9 10 8 6 4 2

Fern Press, an imprint of Vintage, is part of the
Penguin Random House group of companies

Vintage, Penguin Random House UK, One Embassy Gardens,
8 Viaduct Gardens, London SW11 7BW

penguin.co.uk/vintage
global.penguinrandomhouse.com

Penguin
Random House
UK

First published by Fern Press in 2026

Typeset in 11.1/15.2pt Calluna by Six Red Marbles UK, Thetford, Norfolk
Printed and bound in Great Britain by Clays Ltd, Elcograf S.p.A.

The authorised representative in the EEA is Penguin Random House Ireland,
Morrison Chambers, 32 Nassau Street, Dublin D02 YH68

A CIP catalogue record for this book is available from the British Library

ISBN 9781911717539

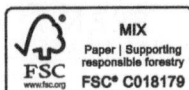

For Eugene

Contents

How inappropriate to call this planet Earth, when clearly it is Ocean.

Arthur C. Clarke

SHORE

I

Clear of all other moorings, ties, and places that might have been easier to reach, we had come to a beach on a curve so lazy it was not so much a curve as the slow rendition of the curvature of the earth drawn by hand. There were no high buildings, so if you wanted, you could track the beach entirely by turning your head from one side to the other the full extent of the neck until it clicked.

Yellow sand. Blue sky.

Yellow sand. Blue sky.

Not at all warm.

Twice a day the sound of a bell played across the bay. Clear or muffled as the wind took it.

Loosely tacked on to the bay was a scattered strip of clapboard houses. It was an eccentric little town once you got to know it, though from the waterfront you couldn't tell. Each building was two storeys or three. Nothing blocked the sun and wind. On the beach, we were exposed.

Bending down, I pulled on Garland's hood. Sun and wind both burn so I was careful to put his hood back on each time it fell but it fell all the time, so putting on and falling off were mostly the action of the morning. The wind whipped the sand into a million stings. Gloves are no good in sand. His fingers were red and his cheeks red too, like I had slapped him.

Your daddy must be very proud of you! the hostess had said to the sleepy boy after the long flight. *My daddy is dead* said the boy and the hostess had turned her face away quickly so that he could not see how it looked but not quite quick enough.

A plane over the Atlantic gives no perspective on the world. Land or sea, it makes no difference. Below us, darkness lay as thrown in great loose sheets. The sea was without form and void. We flew for hours – economy – Garland curled in his seat in fitful sleep and me beside him, upright in low-grade physical suspension. Cabin lights glowed pale in honour of the sleeping cargo. Somewhere in the blue core of the midnight watch, my leg went dead and turned to meat. I kicked the leg awake along the narrow aisle. It had been a journey of maximum discomfort. They always are. *Please God make me not fly again.*

Yet such is the amnesia of flight (it is a bracket that contains nothing) that on arrival, it was forgotten like it had never been, and so it seemed as if we fetched up lightly here on the rim, in a wooden house built on sand at the edge of a slow bay, halfway down a parade of similar wooden houses: floors, decks, walls, stairs; all made of wood. Our house was called Small Paynes or Small Paynes Landing depending on who was doing the naming, and it was as well disposed to the sea as it was to the land, as if its purpose was simply to be a

6

passing place, a halt, from one state of dry, to another one of wet. Houses in the parade were different but looked related in the way that people in extended families look related – same jawline, bones and shanks cast in the same mould. The walls were made from cedar shingle overlapping, like scales from the costume of a fish. To see one of the buildings laid out bare in the sun was immediately to understand how it was made even if you had never got near to building a house yourself. A child could make such a house. Anyone could do it.

It seemed right that a house on a beach with its piles extending over the water at high tide should be made of wood. The place was halfway gone to being a boat, so lightly did it hold the shore and the sea, ever-in-motion, that swept and dumped sand along the periphery all hours of the day and night, scourged the bay and made the position of the house feel slighter and even more provisional than it might have been. I looked around to get my bearings. So this was where we had come.

A wooden house is a made-up thing. Pretend, like a house in a story. We were not used to wood. We came from the city. Our background was solid, brick and urban: pavements and tarmac underfoot, dry-cleaners, traffic, kerbs and cycle lanes, the lot. Concrete is unforgiving but at least with concrete you know where the ground is. It does not shift. This was a town built on a sand bar set parallel against the ocean. Shifting was fully in its nature.

Wood by the sea is friable, like houses are not meant to be. It can go one way or another, salt and soften, split and atomise and polish down to chips and grains, or it might remain whole, but become over time loosened, unmoored and perhaps one morning after a storm, parts of it be recovered along the coast as so much debris, bobbing timber, chewed and spat out, ready to be refashioned into another structure

7

further down. There were always other structures along that stretch in need of parts. It was relentless. The sea is a machine.

Small Paynes Landing was a collage made of wood. In a wood economy, what belonged to one home might readily be transposed and incorporated into another. That is the way of things. Everything built might be rebuilt, improved upon, patched up and added to as wind and weather dictated. All the buildings, the jetties, the stairs and little decks looked like they had been fashioned from other jetties, other stairs and little decks elsewhere. A wooden house embraces its own instability. The tidal zone brewed up a bond, a lively belt of demarcation between the houses and the shore, with elements that pertained to both left to evolve and merge in the shadows that were marked in dark green and blue and black under the berths and in the lazy currents that moved beneath each step and pier. It made a rich penumbra, an undertow where things might live and grow and blossom, in warmth but out of direct sun. Garland on arrival could see instantly that this was an area worth exploring. He made straight for the water's edge.

At the shore, the afterlife of objects is exposed. There is no hiding place for things or people under the sun. The bay, shaped like a spoon, caught what the Atlantic carried in and held it close. *The green plastic shutter of a large verandah shorn from its casing. A section of FloPlast-quality PVC downpipe in anthracite. A yellow bumper snapped in two.* These objects would be found miles further down snagged on the coast as flotsam. The sea will not hold them. And when they fetch up elsewhere, what happens then?

All this and more I thought in the first hour. The sun was already high.

In Sunday school – there had been a song that went:

> The foolish man built his house upon the sand.
> The foolish man built his house upon the sand.
> The foolish man built his house upon the sand.
> And the house on the sand fell down.

On the last word, the children standing in the circle stamped their feet together – *So!* That was the best, the bit we loved. To glory in the fool's downfall. The wise man, of course – verse two – built his house upon the rock. *How? How did he lay the foundations?*

Within the economy of Sunday school, all metaphors were tightly plotted. There were no summer houses and no second homes. In the alignment of the moral compasses of six-year-olds, nothing was wasted: *the man, the sand, the house, the rock, the floods, the rain.* Everything had meaning, and the meanings were solid and so much clearer then than meanings ever are now or will be again. It was as if the children themselves were small, improvised structures to be tinkered with and worked on slowly week by week, tapped at and reinforced in work of careful bricolage. Back then we felt the value of this labour going on obscurely as a form of pride. The work was slow and steady, proceeding weekly through songs and games and Bible stories under the attentive eyes of adults. It meant that we were worth it.

The chorus I remember went:

> The rain came down and the floods came up.
> The rain came down and the floods came up.

The rain came down and the floods came up.
And the house on the sand fell down.

A house on sand was clearly not to be trusted. But looking at Small Paynes Landing on that first morning in the white lens of the sun, you could only admire its flaws and degradations. Here was a house that had gone with all possible flows, and that must be the secret to its longevity. This was building as endeavour, as process and evolution. The treads were rubbed smooth and slightly bowed through years of use. Seagrass had roughed it through the piles to bind everything that lay beneath tighter together. The coat of algae that stretched like bespoke baize under the deck was an impeccable shade of pristine green. Garland poked his finger through its viridescence, delighted at the luminosity of its mass and how it clotted round his fingers in viscous, alien, loving strands. Small Paynes had stood in the same spot for over a hundred years, from when the sea was awash with fish – more Bible stories – and the Portuguese community who had come to colonise the town in the not so far past for its abundant catch, was thriving. In all that time it hadn't fallen down, and if you knew how to look, you might read the life of a house in coats of paint like rings in a tree. *How long does history need to be anyway?*

It was impossible to gauge its colour. The sun steals the body of colour away and leaves its ghost. Colour is unfixable. It plays tricks. Colour is molecular, refractive: it is shades and pigments, coverage, shine, opacity. Colour is culture and chemistry. It is name. It is the making of one clear choice over another. Early storms hitting the bay by night, sun baking its rim by day, had taken the original paint long since down from its native shade. Subsequent paintings had seen a muting to the rinse that remained after dissolving all other colour into salt. The sinks in a restaurant kitchen in the early hours came close to this near-nothing shade: a greasy swill, cut through with food and sluiced with sauce that shone in the double basins under the lights. It was vegetable, animal and mineral. Blue and olive, brown and mauve, grey, black and mustard yellow. At nineteen I worked the late shift in a restaurant kitchen, cash in hand. I knew the colour of that water well. It was zombie water, alive and dead.

The capacity of a wooden house set by the sea to absorb water is limitless. Spray turned the wood black as gangrene. The sun blanched it back to bone. Sodium chloride was the agent, its residue weathered down to mouse or vole. And like an animal, we found that if you stroked the house along its grain on a dry day, it was soft and warm. All this and more I learned in the second hour.

In another life, I thought we might own Small Paynes. Maybe we could live there. We didn't have enough money or even sight of enough money, but it was winter, there were no other contenders around and here we were. You have to seize your moments where you can. *Another life . . . That's what we were after.*

Yellow sand. Blue sky.

Yellow sand. Blue sky.

All clear. Not at all warm.

Garland was getting restless.

The wind was laced with ice. The edges of my vision were the edges of the horizon. The horizon was a wire. The dome of the sky oscillating against the bowl of the sea trapped the super-white, hostile sun and trained its beam down on us. The combination of cold and bright could be spectacularly cruel. Or maybe it was ordinarily cruel. I fix Garland's hood for the thousandth time and straighten back into the wind.

This is why we have come! I shout to him, but he is off. Already gone too far away to hear me.

2

The dreamlike state had ended abruptly on arrival. At customs, we were picked from the line and ushered into a small, blank room. The border lady has a Polish name, but she is American and I would do well to keep in mind, a member of the US Customs and Border Protection Team. It is embroidered on her badge. For us the day has only just begun. For her it is continuous with night. Her shift has been going on for many hours already. Without moving anything in her face, I see she is not pleased.

The border lady is looking at our papers. I am looking at the straight crease in her parted hair. It makes a rift, a great divide across her scalp, raked with a steel comb, neat as a line in a Zen garden made by an attentive gardener. I bring my full awareness carefully to this line, the left and right of it. Yes, or is it no?

This is your son?

Yes, this is my son.

He doesn't have your name.

He has his father's name.

Do you have his birth certificate?

Here . . .

She takes the crumpled paper, folded in half.

You are travelling just the two of you?

Yes, we are the two.

This isn't a proper sentence but seems to express who we are.

We were three.

Sam was dead.

Now we are two.

My mouth is dry. I swallow to get my voice into the right register. A popped eardrum is drawing my attention. The room seemed hushed at first, but now I notice how it's filled in subtle ways with polyphonic sounds you sense rather than hear. The scanners in the concourse, the drone of air conditioning, the hum of the ceiling vent. The printer, even in dormant mode is audible. In the arrivals hall, information is heavily compressed. Outside, the line moves slowly. *Entry. Entry denied. Entry. Entry denied.* Chaos is barely held in check. The sounds are the opposite of any music, expanding even while airborne to stop the ears and fill up the little drums like glue. It's warm. I feel a headache coming on.

Are you on vacation? she asks.

How could we be on vacation?

I make a guess.

Yes.

It's an unusual name, she says flatly, looking at me as if for the first time.

Somewhere in the far past, I might have told her, I had

ancestors from over here who handed the name down, sometimes skipping a generation and then resurfacing, to gift it carefully like an ornament still in tissue, unwrapped from a cardboard box at Christmas. *Garland* it was. Garland was always going to be Garland. But I want her to know nothing about me.

Yes, I say again.

She hands our papers back. The interview is over. We both turn to Garland. His face is neutral, flat and open. His hair churned up with sleep. We had nothing to hide but we were kept in the room a quarter-hour and made to feel that whatever our world view was, it was unwelcome, and we should keep it to ourselves, and we would be well advised to leave the country as soon as we could, and even though we had no idea what we were doing there, under no circumstances should we try to extend our stay.

We had arrived at speed. The whole thing had been organised and booked in about three weeks. We could not have done it ourselves. Could not do anything at that point ourselves. We did not have capacity. Dina had invited us, told us about Small Paynes, and said not to worry, she would arrange it all, be there to meet us, pick us up, drive us and house us, the whole thing. I read each of her emails over many times to make sure I understood what she was saying and asked my friends to check them for me to be extra sure. I could not afford to get things wrong. There was no margin for error. A misunderstanding or a missed connection would mean taking a decision by myself. That could not happen.

Dina had sent us a picture of a red cardinal by way of invitation and though we never set eyes on the bird the whole time we were there – *I still have not seen a red cardinal* – it had been enough. A red cardinal is a red cardinal. An invitation is an invitation. And time, well, time is just time. There was nothing to be done with it. Locating ourselves like stowaways inside the lives of others rather than trying to live through the coming months ourselves seemed as good a decision as any.

I was not wrong. As promised, Dina and her girlfriend Maeve were waiting for us at the airport. It was dark. Excessive kindness should be flagged and given fair warning. It can be hard as cruelty unless you are prepared and their faces, open smiles, their arms around us and the heady smell of the warm hire car, almost felled me before we began. Dina gave us a day or so to uncurl at her place after the flight, and then, installing us again in the car with Garland strapped in a seat in the back, she tilted her head, put her foot on the gas and overtook everything in sight on the turnpike for a long three hours until we reached the coast, while she talked non-stop the while, and a recurring laugh rattled round in her throat. She talked about the past, our friends in common, her present life with Maeve, the future they had planned. She kept on talking. She talked so freely it was bewildering. As if a life could simply be continuous, not snapped in two. Dina and Maeve were talking so I didn't have to. This was a kindness too. One of so many.

I could see Garland in the rear-view mirror. He was a boy bewitched. Not by the talk, in which he had no interest, but by the journey speeding past. His eyes were black holes that sucked in everything around him, the glittering road, the lights that flashed between the pines, the monster articulated trucks that roared and vanished in the same white dragon-breath of fuel as she overtook them at speed in the outside lane. Dina the driver had set the universe in motion, but Garland was its presiding, self-appointed god. There was nothing about the journey that was not fantastical, and not made for him alone to enjoy.

Garland was in the long *vehicle* phase of boyhood. He'd fallen hard for machines and could seem at that stage to love them more than people. I knew what he was thinking. He *was* the car, its chrome, its body, its velocity and we, the women, were his acolytes and there to serve. *Go faster* he whispered. *Faster.* He repeated this request on a loop for miles, kicking his legs, ever more deranged, like a boy needing to piss, and once, when he did need to piss, we barely made it to a stop in time. Afterwards, we stuffed him with crisps and warm ham peeled from plastic sheets in dampened slices. Only later, as the light faded, did he go quiet. He slept.

The last few miles we left the roaring highway to join a lumpy, looping road that dipped in and out of scrappy wooded land and opened up to track the naked shoreline, until the pines, the holm oaks and the elms thinned out, rough dunes began, and the road ran into a little town that ended in the sea and went no further because there was no further to go.

Some towns come without a guidebook. Or on arrival, the map fits on a single page. You search with interest, looking for clues but there are none. The map bleeds into whiteness.

It was a small town, more a settlement. The sky was just becoming stellar. The sun not packed away. A new moon pinned in the pale air waited its turn above the houses arranged in single file along the shoreline with the horizon as their constant fix and anchor. One of these was ours.

I could see Garland, now awake, freed from the car and running circles in the icy air. Dina and Maeve were stretching, starting to unpack the bags, their laughter mixing in companionable clouds of breath above their heads. A little gold dog trotted down the street like a merry gunslinger heading into town and when it passed, it stopped to leave a little golden poo, a welcome gift that matched the colour of its coat and matched the sand that blurred away the strip of beach to blend it with the road and soften the line between the two. I noticed all these things but could not until a long time later point to or name the feeling that arose. As if I saw the scene unnaturally close, close enough to note the fine grain of everything, but at the same time as information that was hazy, disconnected, vague. The near had flipped to a setting far away, while the far had landed thick and fast upon us. I was an outsider, present in the scene if only to record it, to note the warmth that radiated from the living things, the proximity of the houses to the sea, the way they jutted out onto the beach on piles and how in the evening light the air seemed filled with yellow dust that fell like the slowest ever pollen down to settle, making each separate surface incandescent, lightly glistered with sand and polished to a sensual purpose yet to be understood.

The town was old and yellow-gold, filtered and cast through golden glass. Maybe this was how it was to be. To see the world at one remove. From now on, this landscape and all the ones that were to follow, would be experienced by me alone and no element of it, nothing large or small that took place as point of record – the dog, the sand, the sea, the sun – would be seen by him again. Not Garland. Not even Garland. That was a complex thought. Too sharp. Too bright. Best not to stare at it directly. I picked up my bags and followed them inside.

Our apartment was on the second floor, except that there were no floors at Small Paynes but rooms that were built off landings and half-landings linked by the stairs and stilts that made up the whole. The half-landing was the main architectural feature. Nothing would have been built without it. They allowed the stairs to turn on such a narrow footprint it was like building tentatively into air. You went up a certain way and then you turned, went up a bit more, hesitated, turned again and each turn gave the house a further aspect of uncertainty, as if as well as being built on sand, the stairs had been constructed on a whim while out on a stroll in advance of the actual building and left to find their way up to each room by chance. One unit was set so casually upon another, provisionally balanced in interim arrangement until such time as it might be properly secured and if that time was still to come, no matter. This was building as speculation. Small Paynes was not so much a house, more a collection of cabins one on top of the other, looking out to sea. The stairs were open, wooden, single balustrade, and slippery when wet. That was where, on the second day, just as we were waking to our new surroundings, Garland fell.

Throw the camera down the stairs and let it run. Slow the frame rate. Play it back.

As a film it was primitive, but effective. *Have you watched a child fall down the stairs?* All the way I tracked him, saw the whole sequence A–Z, from first misstep to head-hit-post and could swear to the malleability of time. It took *whole minutes*. I had time to notice how he rolled, how his body flipped twice, how he had seemed in retrospect to have launched himself with deliberation, something like joy into the air, rather than slip. This was falling as assertion rather than omission. As if in his excitement at the bright new world with its blue untroubled rim laid out afresh before him, he thought to leap.

I had time to notice everything and react in every way except to stop him. It took longer to watch him fall than it takes to read a description of him falling. He did not die – *that would have been the end of reading* – his forehead hit the post at the bottom and I saw that in slow motion too. The rebound, the little bounce once, the rubbery shock to the neck. All the way down I screamed. That's what Garland said later anyway. I had no memory of it.

Why were you screaming?
Because you were falling.
Who were you screaming at?

It was a good point. Dina and Maeve were nowhere near. They lived on the other side of town. At Small Paynes Landing there was no one else to hear us. He came to no harm and the giant egg on his forehead spread over days into an antique bruise of finely blended, subtle colours, so delicate it looked hand-painted. I took two chairs and taped them tight across the gap to make a barricade.

In the fridge there was milk, butter, jam, and the thin, white, sweetened stuff that is American bread. A carton of orange juice. Coffee. That would be breakfast then.

3

As introduction to her book of poems *Geography III* (1976), Elizabeth Bishop chose a lesson of the kind meant to be learned by heart, from a child's primer, *First Lessons in Geography*.

> Lesson I
>
> What is Geography?
> A description of the earth's surface.
> What is the earth?
> The planet or body on which we live.
> What is the shape of the earth?
> Round, like a ball.
> Of what is the Earth's surface composed?
> Land and water.

I liked this formulation. *Race you to the edge!* I shout to Garland.

*

Garland doesn't go to Sunday school. I did. At Sunday school I listened to the stories about how the world was made. Learned about the divisions and separations in the beginning, the laying out of the world into zones one from another, the separation of the water from the air and the land from the water, the distribution of the firmament into a place of stars, another one of sea, another of gas, another of heat and stone. I did not hear these things just once, but many times, in many years, with other children, sat in groups in plain, wood-panelled halls, through words and stories, crayons, paints and pictures, songs, interpretations, degrees of emphasis and imaginative spark.

And the earth was without form – comma – *and void.*

And the earth was without form and void.

I did not learn these stories on their own, to the exclusion of the other stories, long-form ones that glossed over the need for the world to be arrived at in seven days, narratives with ample time for trilobites to generate and thrive, ichthyosaurs to come and go, for meteorites to hit and fossils to bed down in rock over the long haul, for ice ages to overlap, and aeons of time, as shown in all my Natural History books as separate, solid, colour-coded, bands with charismatic names, Precambrian, Mesozoic, Cenozoic, to segue into one another. The stories did not preclude each other. And in the Nature books that laid out how the world was understood back then, I noticed how the distinctions between phenomena were always clearly drawn and marked. Where there was any blurring of the boundaries between the states of things, like as not that meant disruption, friction – clear and present danger. At the edges, is instability. Rock that turns liquid under pressure will flow as molten lava. A tide that recedes and does not return, signals a tsunami. Those who can read the warning signs run for high ground. Those who do not, may die. A fierce storm could carve a brand-new beach in a single night and deposit another somewhere further down the coast. Ice that failed to form as usual on a lake in winter spelled change the following year. I knew those stories too, about the material world and its wild, opposing forces, but the accounts of the void and how it was originally without form and how form was made, stayed in my head. It was the language. It is always the language. *And darkness was on the face of the deep . . .* It still is. The deep is still where darkness is.

And within these cosmographic schemes of separation, of one state divided from another, being a child who loved to draw, who thought that pictures mattered and cared a great deal about the shape and feel of things, I would look to the edges of those pictures where form rose out of formless, and pay attention to the boundaries where two realms met as neighbours and one zone impinged directly against another. In any depiction, where two things touch, something must happen. A line has to be drawn. You can't ignore it. A perimeter will always be a contested zone, a site of resistance, or a potential problem. Two of these boundaries in particular took my interest. The point where sea meets land. The point where water meets the sky. The shore. And the horizon.

Many land borders are divisions we create ourselves, mostly through violence, with consequences handed on for generations. The edge of the sea is not one of them. As such, it is to be respected. The horizon is not a place, but it is a line. The shore, though sometimes called so, is not a line, but it is a place.

After he died, the Earth – *Round like a ball* – continued to spin.

*

In my remembering, this is how it went. In the blank space that followed his father's death, I took Garland across the Atlantic. If you'd asked why, I would not then have known, but now I might say this. Death puts you at the centre of a story in the full glare of its heat and light. When faced with the ocean, we are decentred. At the shore, we will never be the main event. We are peripheral. The sea is good on indifference. It rises to the occasion. We went to the sea.

Garland was four and I was forty-four. Two is the smallest family. Two was barely a family at all. I was aware of its precarity as much as I was aware of anything: what to eat, where to go next, the weather. My mind was stuck on three. Three was the shape we made. There is little space between one and two. No room. To work things out, you need numbers, more elements at play, otherwise all you have is anecdote, conjecture – *mere conjecture* as we sometimes call it, to emphasise how light it is, how little weight it carries. You cannot extrapolate from two. Not enough data. With two, nothing gets lost in the mix. There is no mix.

On the beach at Small Paynes, seen from a distance, Garland and I were double-budded, the far and near of us wrapped in our coats, entangled to seem at times a single form. Everything that would happen between us would happen out in the open. It would be seen. Yet many things go better un-regarded. That I knew. Children need their own horizons and space enough to view them. Two was a sealed formation. From A to B and back again. We were inseparable. Space would have to be made between us. Neither of us was remotely ready.

I am not Mediterranean. The Aegean is a mystery to me, as is the Black Sea, the Sargasso, and the Adriatic. I am unfamiliar with the Pacific. I don't know these waters. When I think of the ocean – I live in the city, I think of the ocean often – it is the Atlantic first and foremost, the Atlantic I return to. The Atlantic is the eighth wonder of the world, a giant maw that holds two continents apart and splits the West stone cold along its middle. It is atrocious, fearsome, wild. *Stick or twist. Stay or go.* The Atlantic is the one to cross.

A coast is a line to set yourself against. It is a buffer. A coast says *STOP!* and *GO NO FURTHER!* Going further usually entailed some form of risk: swimming, drowning, shipwreck or sharks, forms of self-sabotage. *The sill of a window. The lip of a ledge. The spill of a cliff. The sheer steps down.* In my imagining, the edge was a cartoon, a set-up, a sheer drop from which Garland might fall. Garland had fallen once already upon arrival.

Even in calm weather, a coast is a placeholder for the unstable. It is the point of maximum opposition. Land and water. Big and binary. Clumsy and cosmic. Here the land folds, the earth strips back and lays its operations bare. Pools form in one place and basins drain away in another. Tides, wharfs, gulfs, creeks, deltas, bays, inlets, and overflows. Silt from every river that flows into the sea is carried out as cargo, freighted with mud and sand and shells and boats and bits of barge, the skeletons of tiny creatures and the corpses of bigger ones. This is the sea at work. There is no end to anything. The beach at Small Paynes was a just a blip, millennia in the making, where sea took land and mauled it, hand over hand, wave after tiny wave, inch by inch and grain by grain in ancient assault and spat it back. The shore is where the fabric of the material world gets torn. From cliffs to rocks to sand to spume, the process only goes one way. Everything is changed – destroyed – or carried off.

*

I am not romantic, that should be clear by now. I am a prag-matist. I look at the facts as they fall. It was never a conscious decision not to jump or swim – people swimming too far out just make me anxious – but more mundane, much less dramatic. To go to the coast is simply to stall, lock to the line of the horizon, watch, and wait it out to see what happens. At the Atlantic, all decisions are held in flux. You brace yourself, your arms wrapped tight across your chest while your face burns in the sun, or your body chills in the wind. You can't hold this position forever, or even for very long. It's all too cold, too mad, too bright, too bad, too sad, too fleeting. And when you turn back and head again inland, for food or warmth or company or shelter, the hope, the small hope, was that you too might be changed. Whether this was fun for Garland I had no idea. I did not think to ask him. Garland was along for the ride.

To say yes had been an instinctive move. The first of many. I made a guess. I guessed it would be good to go as far away as possible from where we began. If you start out somewhere on the map, pick anywhere, and keep on going, at some point, in some configuration, eventually, you arrive at the sea. That's just geography. The sea gets everywhere and all about. Small Paynes Landing, curved like a clasp, seemed far enough. The place made little sense as land, hard to configure in your mind or even to recall with any sureness once you had left. Isolate but not in fact an island, it was a hook, a spit, an afterthought left behind by waves. The place called out for reclamation.

We are running away. There! I said it, not aloud, but in my head where I said most things. There was no one to say it to apart from Garland and I was not sure how much sense it made to him. What I wanted and what he wanted were closely aligned but not identical. Garland needed me even more now, entirely. I needed him the same. These piggyback desires had got us, me, the boy, his buggy and as much luggage as we could carry, onto a plane across the Atlantic. I guessed again. Meeting his needs, I thought, for the time being, would take care of mine. Mine were obscure. As a journey it had no real object. A holiday was not in question. We did not want to be on holiday. It was a desire framed wholly in negative – not to remain at home. H is for hospital, hospice and home. Those were the markers of our lives for months. We moved between them. A long-haul flight is a strenuous way to avoid being at home. As a response to excess, it was excessive. It was not stupid though. Death had smashed us. When under attack, *move!*

The sea may be indifferent to me, but I am not indifferent to it. On the beach we took what we were given: a sensation so actual that it could best be likened to a solid object. The silver of the sea, the low white waves like the edges of a battered pie tin beaten into frills. Add in the pink sun, late now, that fell on the right, to inflame its opposite number, the blue, so that the clouds – ice palaces, stacked subgroups of ghosts, whatever pictures took your fancy – stood out against it uncommonly precise. Roll that sensation up into a ball and lob it hard back against the sun. A hit! My throat constricts with pleasure. It is the end of the second day. I look around for Garland to share it with him. He sees it too. What thoughts he forms around it I do not know.

4

When asked in an interview who his audience was, the artist Felix Gonzalez-Torres replied, *Ross. The public was Ross. The rest of the people just come to the work*. It's a hard sentence but a good one. An audience of one is enough. Ross was Ross Laycock, his long-term lover, who died of Aids-related complications in 1991, as five years later, he would also die.

Under my bed I have one of his prints rolled up in a tube. I know it's there. I don't need to put it on the wall to think about it. I didn't have to buy it. It's a broadsheet image of the sea in black and white, one that was free to take from his stack print series: Felix Gonzalez-Torres, *"Untitled"* (1991), offset print on paper, endless copies. In the gallery the piles made squared-off bulks, austere and low, sharp edged enough so you could cut yourself. The piles went down and were replenished by the attendants every evening to a certain height in readiness for morning. The tide comes in. The tide goes out again. The condition of the work was that it would never run dry.

A water column is an imaginary monument. It goes all the way down: *epipelagic*; *mesopelagic*; *bathypelagic*; *abyssopelagic*. Felix Gonzalez-Torres, *"Untitled"* (1991) had none of a monument's usual conditions, being made of paper and subject to change.

And to lose your audience of one? That is the whole sea and its depths.

It was true that in the months after, I should not have driven. Grief is a car crash in itself and we should all be wary of decisions taken after a bereavement but this one seemed simple, slight enough to risk. Taking a right off Walmer Road behind a white van that blocks my view of all oncoming traffic, I make a decision that requires no thought, and takes less than no time to do. *Go*.

A car picking up speed to beat the lights screams in behind me, burning my tail – or is it my face? I am so far upended in its wake, I cannot tell. The man's rage is a flare and in the suspended second that follows not being hit, looped so casually between one state of being, *hit*, and the other, *not*, I see his mouth twist into the shape of a curse that flames in my direction to set us both on fire. The just are righteous and the righteous are just. The skin of his car is hot and dry and silver-thin, processed to a tight foil sheen. Up close, it is the skin of a fighter jet and just as deadly.

Outwardly nothing had happened. There's nothing to see. I keep driving but hold the sound of the smash and what it would have been like in my head like a cup filled to the brim. I try to hold it steady as I drive, now slowly and so responsibly along the road but the sound, the terrible, absent sound has turned the whole car into a clanging bell. It's so hot and loud inside the bell that I can't think. Condensation drips from its rim. I have to pull over. No one comes running. Nothing has even happened. I am illuminated but no one has seen me. Shock is just not visible.

I couldn't say exactly that I took more care afterwards, but maybe I did. Maybe there was a small step change, some click or movement, one notch up in the direction of greater responsibility. I had started seeing a counsellor by that time, mainly to cry but sometimes in gaps, to speak, and was gratified to see how seriously she took the story. Comprehension often falls well behind the curve. Sometimes you have to see the reaction your stories have on others to make sense of them yourself.

Slow down your decision-making.

Under stress your reactions are impaired.

Take extra time to think.

Care in everything – crossing a road, boiling a kettle – everything.

I was not killed and nor was he. No thanks to me.

I didn't tell her then about the other times, the time on the roof, the time at the window. The times when no one else was involved. Nothing happened those times either. Those were just thoughts and thoughts are not events. Thoughts are a different category entirely. They matter less. And anyway, I was not ready to tell her these things.

Felix Gonzalez-Torres
"Untitled", 1991
Print on paper, endless copies
7 inches at ideal height × 45¼ ×
    38½ inches (original paper size)
Installed in *Portraits*, *Plots* and *Places:*
    The Permanent Collection Revisited.
    Walker Art Center, Minneapolis,
    MN. 7 Jan. 1992–6 Mar. 1994

5

Though faced each morning with the sea unrolled and laid out flat, at Small Paynes Landing we spent the longest time in the bath. This was unexpected. Bathrooms, it seems, are consolation to the bereaved. The bath is a proxy for the coffin, or the womb, whichever is the closer. The pleasures of a bath are slow. The sea, bright and dazzling, was quick as a razor. It was far too cold to swim.

At Small Paynes, each day of that first week I took a bath and sometimes two. The aim was not so much to pass the time as stop it dead, have done with it. The bath was somewhere fixed to put myself: a space, quite small and circumscribed that I could give my full attention to. A boat.

In the bath I would lie still, holding the water level static, rising my belly a little mound above the surface to make of my stomach a pale circuit of survival. My belly was an island on which no one would drown as long as I kept my breath under control. As a child I did this happily, testing the limits of my power to make even the water submit to my will. Now it was urgent, so I took my time. Slowed down my breathing till there was hardly a ripple. *How long?* Not long enough. The water turned white gold, then cold. Only Garland's fussing for my attention, for food or company or play, the things that only I could muster for him, would drag me out.

In the bath you flatten and loosen. Flesh breaks out in pimples, red, white, blue. The organs rest. The heart slows in its chamber. Pierre Bonnard painted his wife Marthe de Méligny, over and over in the bath. Bonnard in his bathroom paintings, sliced her down into a sliver the colour of margarine and squeezed her into the narrow space between the tub and the edge of the picture. In the bath she is compressed, in paint compressed again. Her sallow yellow seeps through blue, bleeds into green. I wish she'd gone the other way, to liquid. After so many hours of standing, staring, dabbing and smearing at the woman inside the tub, prone and still enclosed, now cold – Bonnard might have set her free as wash, as gesture, to spill and spread until she took over the canvas and swept out of the frame altogether. All that air and all that water. All that paint and all that light, rolling out of the apartment, down the stairs and onto the street. *Marthe has left the building!* Paris in flood. That would have been something to see.

Showers don't do death justice. A shower is clean. A shower is the whole thing washing away. We didn't want that. Experience had cost us dear, and for that reason should be twice held close. Forgetting was the last thing we wanted. I never thought of drowning. The coast was clear. The sea was right outside the door, across the floor and down three flights of stairs. There was no one to check on us exactly. Apart from Dina and Maeve and the friends of Dina and Maeve who stuck out the winter, we met few people. The woman who sold fruit, the young librarian called Sheila, the massage lady. Alessandro from the bar. It was the slowest time of year. Most people were out of town, in Florida they said, or Mexico, that's where they went, or else they stayed at home. The locals we met in the street were wrapped up warm against the cold. When people said *Hi*, their breath caught in the wool of their scarves and hung at their mouths like a gate. It was warmth we craved and a space that would hold you close and neat so if you shook you made no sound at all. The house, shut fast against the wind, was such a place. The bath, another. The bath at Small Paynes was a holding space, a proxy stop beside the ocean. A decompression chamber that marked our transition from an old life into a new. I craved its pale enamel form. We were in limbo. The next life, whatever shape it might assume, was not yet clear. At least we could be sure of going into it very clean.

Sometimes in the bath, I'd sing to Garland. He liked the sound of my voice whichever way it came and was not yet of an age to shut me down. That would come later.

> Oh Captain tell me true
> Does my sailor sail with you?
> No, he does not sail with me.
> He sleeps at the bottom of the sea.
>
> What did the deep sea say?
> Tell me what did the deep sea say?
> Moaned and groaned and splashed and foamed.
> Rolled on its weary way.

The bathroom was small. If Garland managed to get into the bath before me – some days it was a fight – our habit then would be to hang out for a while, me on the floor with my back pressed hard against the radiator as if to fuse my spine onto its grooves – *I could never be warm enough* – and him in the bath, playing with soap and a row of plastic dinosaurs lined up like sheep along its rim. In the bath, he knew he had my attention fully. Once we got settled in, it was a good place to talk.

Now he's asking me what colour is. What is it made of? *What is red?* Pressing his palms hard against his eyes he blacks out deep magenta shapes stuck through with pins of red and pink and green that are still there in front of him when he takes his hands away and stares, excited, round the room to will it back to focus. *Light*, I say. *Reflected light*. Then after a pause. W*aves*. I can tell these are not the answers he wants. Waves churn ceaselessly outside the window. *That's not what I mean*, he says. *What is it really?* What do I tell him? That the sea is not made of blue and the sun not really yellow? That colour is not physical at all but neurological, a construct sparking in the brain somewhere between the mind and eye? That colour is not real?

Or should I say that waves are real, yes, and light is real, yes, but colour has no reality outside our need and comprehension of it. That snakes see infrared to track the warm-blooded shapes of prey. That bees use ultraviolet to navigate the forms of flowers for food. He is insistent. *What is red?* I have become more stupid on this, and every other question. How is he going to learn anything with only me to teach him? Sam was always good with words. He could do carmine and crimson and all the other colours. Sam would sink a red berry into a bowl of porridge for Garland to discover: spoon up a sunny blob of egg and wobble it to make him laugh before he ate it. *What is colour?* Now I would have to name them all

44

myself. He wants me to induct him into its mysteries and this is just the beginning. I am not up to the task. I am not even adequate.

The sea is beyond the colour chart. Outside, I know that in the sea, the red rays are the first to disappear at depth, taking with them the warm tones and all the heat, then after that the cooler shades, the greens, leaving the blues and sunken violets to linger as if made of heavier material lower down. Below that, there is a darkness that still is nothing like *actual black* but constitutes the removal of all concepts of colour beyond the sun. The fish of the abyss have never felt its rays. At depths of 1,000 feet and more, bioluminescence is the only light, which in tone resembles the moon more than the sun, and in the extravagance of the creatures that produce it, the moon at carnival, kitted out in the most fantastical of costumes.

He's on a roll now, eager to have me tell him everything I know. *How old is the sea's water?* he asks. Enough. I have enough. I'm tired. I am saved by a violent shift in his attention. Seizing the sponge, he makes a sudden, swooshing noise and with a splash, sweeps all the dinosaurs in cosmic final reckoning into the water. It is *done*. Later, once he went to bed, I would return. I'd give the bath a second life and step into it myself to lie there in his water. And that would be another day gone.

Back home, Garland's favourite exhibit in the Science Museum was the video on liquefaction. When an earthquake hits, soil below the water table can become saturated and lose its grip. In such a heightened state, it flows like liquid, taking boats, cars, houses, schools and whole hillsides with it. Sometimes on museum trips, being mortal tired of childcare, I steeled myself as personal challenge to take in *nothing*

45

at all, but liquefaction would break through my defences. Liquefaction always got my attention. Dissolution was a state I had sympathy with.

Once, another child – not mine – interrupted the video by screaming and arcing in his father's arms as if to throw himself violently, head backwards to the ground in an act of blatant self-annihilation. The father was calm but resolute. He simultaneously restrained and ignored his child, while watching the video to its end alongside Garland, who sat beside him, gripped.

There are three types of tectonic plate movement: Divergent, Convergent and Transform. Most seismic activity occurs at these plate boundaries. Later, I heard Garland rehearsing them in the bath, setting the water against the movements of his tummy. He will learn the things he needs well enough. He doesn't need me to teach him.

6

Where did we begin? I don't remember. With birth. That's where it usually starts. And death. Another sort of beginning for those who are left. I am the parent singular. I am the depository and the sink, the reservoir, the sump, the tank. I am the oftentimes still water. I run deep, I run shallow as the mood takes me. This is not a role I would have chosen.

When a parent dies, the twin tributaries that rain down to mix and pool in complex, onward living flow: irrigant, dousing and divergent – stop. The child has memory, yes – like a dry river in summer will keep the form of water. However elemental you may have thought the landscape, however constant, however sure you were of its formation previously, a certain course has been deflected. It is transformed.

Garland's birth was no different from many birthing stories. If you have read others, you may skip it. Before I had a child, I did not have children in my imagination. I did not dream children, nor did I yearn for their potential. I did not miss them in advance. I did not look around for something I did not have. I am not imaginative. In some ways, yes, but not in that way. Imagining a child of my own was impossible, but then again, imagining the child away once he arrived, equally impossible.

The child once born, was evident, but the memory of his birth and the circumstances of him coming into being were not. When I try to recall Garland's birth, it is with effort. Some women have that day etched into the flesh. They can summon it up at will. I have to think it through. Like so many things, his birth has become a form of words. For this, I blame Garland, his native cunning. Throughout his first years, he self-erased as experiment, starting afresh each day in analogue. Rewinding, and renewing, replacing all previous versions, as if in a pre-emptive strike he was spooling himself out, willing me into forgetting him as prelude to letting him go. All children do this, but seen at close range I was in awe of such dexterity. That is the deal. Garland will leave. I must let go.

The early years are an affront to stasis. As he grew, this experimentation changed. It appeared to shift, or because I knew his patterns, became familiar. We got used to each other. He grew towards me and I towards him as he assumed his rightful shape. And as his shape became more rightful, mine became less certain, more incoherent. Vague. Demands were being made and met – or not.

Nine months is long in the life of any animal. Being pregnant is exciting, exhilarating, boring, unnerving and the first time you encounter it, deeply strange. It was going to take roughly the same time whatever I did, so I looked to the other mothers, the live depositories of local knowledge, pregnant, post-pregnant, and long-since pregnant gone. I copied them.

So much is written about pregnancy, yet it remains a state apart. Transient like a journey. Detached as an island. Knowledge is plural. It can be shared. The body is singular. It is a tight float in a small tank.

You wouldn't think a baby could get lost inside a body but the geography of the child on the day of his birth was opaque. Apart from a clear sense of going into labour, there was not much traction or purchase, no evidence of the child's intentions, save for my mysterious belly, prosaic, precarious, and by then simply a burden. We were all under pressure.

Here comes baby, they crowed in the morning at 10 a.m. By 5 p.m., they had stopped crowing and were mainly silent. As the day went on, nurses spent more time on screens and less time looking at me. What the child was doing and where exactly he or she was, I was not sure. There were two fixed points to guide us in, both distinct and standalone. The first was the knowledge that it would end. The second was Sam, the constant one, close at hand and fully present, shifting his weight from side to side. Steady, alert with interest, eyes wide, amazed at the unfolding scene, the birthing of a child, in a Western city, in the full glare of the lights, and at his place within it.

Our little group undulated together for hours, Sam and me and the child-not-being-born; spasmodically, methodically, coming and going, peaking and ebbing, rolling, plateauing, while nothing much seemed to be happening at all. Intimacy and alienation went hand in hand. We did the things we were advised to do. Got into the water. Got out of the water. Walked up the corridor. Down again. Doing and being done to were close-adjacent. The child-coming-into-being was ahead of me at every step, just out of view but on a different orbit, as if we might, by some misfortune even now, fail to align at the appropriate time.

By 3 p.m., I suggested that a caesarean would be just fine and continued to suggest it many times thereafter, but they insisted we keep on going along, so we all kept on going along together, like a tight little team on a tight little ship on open sea.

Twice we snagged. One was the blip of a heartbeat, a glitch, a break in the pattern of the rhythm that had accompanied us so faithfully since morning. The voices in the room dropped lower still. Nurses whispered to each other and to the screens. The door swung ever wider on its hinges. Nameless young doctors came and went. Nobody knocked. And then an hour later – two. The heartbeat cut out a second time. Now comes the green wave. That was the signal to reel us in.

Somewhere in the backwash of the wave that carried us in one continuous, fluid motion, out of the room and into a theatre thronged with people – *where had they been all this time?* – there is a piece of yellow paper with a looping line as signature. A high-water mark. A line that bears the same relationship to my name as a scream bears to my voice. I held a pen. I signed a consent form. I did consent.

It took six minutes from the second dip of Garland's heartbeat to his first airborne cry. A corps de ballet, a swift realignment in the room, a game played out supremely well, gave me a baby so relaxed to make you wonder where he had been the previous nine hours.

Scene One. I am divided. Garland is eel skinny. His eyelashes are the longest I have ever seen on any human and now he's batting them at me. *What does he want?*

7

Looking to find how many versions there were of Piet Mondrian's *Pier and Ocean*, I get stuck on five. *So few!* I thought there would be more. I kept seeing the same one and counting it over again. This is not to be confused with scholarship.

The *Pier and Ocean* drawings are not the same, but they are close, each one the draft of an idea that narrows on its target and disperses. It is a rudimentary scene. There is a kind of pier. The ocean surface flat and spreading. Some are just pencil sketches glued to dog-eared board, near scraps. Others are more substantial, ink on paper. The pier is a clutch of broken lines, some short, some long, but makes its presence felt within the scheme. White splats of gouache wink over a brown or neutral surface. Colour has been left behind. It is a heavily repressed range, a repertoire of plus and minus marks in ink and paint yet fundamentally and mysteriously expansive. There is no dark in *Pier and Ocean*. There is no blue.

There is a version from 1914 that ended up in the Miller Company Collection of Abstract Art, which is pretty scruffy but contains something that might for sure be a pier.

> *Pier and Ocean 1*, Ink and gouache on paper, 50.2 × 62.9. Signed and dated lower right (inside oval): P.M '14 (in New York handwriting) Gift of the artist to Charmion von Wiegand, New York, 1941–1948.

Then the more famous one from 1915, sometimes known as *Sea and Starry Sky*.

> *Pier and Ocean 5*, Charcoal and gouache on paper, 87.9 × 111.7. Glued in late 1941 onto Homasote panel, which was removed in 1968. Signed and dated lower center: P.M '14 (in New York handwriting after the drawing was mounted on the Homasote panel). Purchased from the artist in 1942 through the Valentine Gallery by the Museum of Modern Art, New York.

I didn't know *Homasote* so looked it up. A recycled cardboard known for its robust properties and usefulness in model-making. Cheap and readily available. American.

It is possible to spend a lot of time with *Pier and Ocean*, though some would say there is not much to see. This is Mondrian at the seaside, on the lip of an idea, moving away from anything that might be termed 'scenery'. When he made the drawings, he was an outlier in place and time, staying for several summers just before the outbreak of war in Domburg, a seaside town in Zeeland on the Dutch coast. Zeeland is part of Walcheren, a clump of land that juts into the North Sea, once itself an island

and now a province built out of groups of hills and surrounding islands, connected over time by dykes. Much of it is below sea level. Mondrian knew it well. He was part of a loose community of artist friends converging there, drawn by the flat sands and effervescent light, but it's a harsh place to be. First, there's the beach, bisected all along its length by breakwaters that chop the sand in segments as far as the eye can see. Then, behind the beach, pressed hard against it, the dyke curves round, separating the low sea from the low-lying land and the people who live there from certain inundation. The dyke is the highest point for miles, rubbed raw by the wind, along with anyone who dares to walk its length. The sun has space and more than cumulative force. The sky is uninterrupted light. Nothing gets in its way. Sea in front. Dunes behind. Mondrian walked the beach at night. He sat on the dunes. Swam in the sea. He knew what the sea felt like from the inside.

The *Pier and Ocean* pictures point outwards, to a series that is numberless, like fish fanning across the ocean. That's why I looked for more. From such a vantage, the possibilities are endless. It is a binary language of horizontal and vertical shoals, heading out towards the periphery of your vision.

Zero. One. Zero. Zero. One. One. One. Waves rise in sequence. Fall back again in flows. Light refracts too fast to be decoded. The ocean is never still, too quick to follow with the naked eye. Oscillation is its main mode and scintillation its effect. The depths absorb. The surface resists with force. Light bounces back. Above – below. Air – water. Sun – shade. The sea is just a screen that separates. Beneath it you might vanish. Lose yourself.

Mondrian loved music. He kept a gramophone in every studio he owned and was well known to be a dancer, keen on jazz, and foxtrot, tango, ballroom. He liked to spend nights with friends in dance halls listening to the in-house swing band. With his black suit, black specs and distinctive moves he picked up the nickname Dancing Madonna.

Pier and Ocean is a view from the edge. For Mondrian, it was a moment of close attention from which to launch. He'd got rid of the trees, the dunes, the local church, the actual sea, he wanted none of it; *nothing specific, nothing human*. After the *Pier and Ocean* pictures, the view dissolves and shifts again. The rudimentary pier collapses, falls away. The horizon vanishes into a field of vision that goes on uninterrupted. Titles thin to the drier, more brittle *Composition*.

If *Pier* marks Mondrian's place within the image, a platform from which he could be both the observer of the scene he was describing and inside it, with the proxy of a shadow-self stretching before him, then after *Pier and Ocean*, he went out further still, to make a new set of rules into which he could immerse himself and disappear, clean as a swimmer slips below the surface. Threatened by war in Europe, he went at first to London, then when the nightly bombs began, to America – Manhattan, prime city of the grid and line, to paint the blast of squared-up, syncopated colour that is *Broadway Boogie Woogie*. From the coast to the city, from the edge to the centre. Mondrian crossed the Atlantic.

8

Small Paynes was on a strip of land where the sand stuck out into the ocean like the tongue of a lizard and licked it daily clean of salt. It was a place of summer crush and winter dereliction, of sun and storms, white dunes laced through with ponds, of lone dogs, and holed-up flocks of migrant birds in season. *A colony of wharf houses*, is how an estate agent would describe it, were it up for sale. Summer houses were never part of my existence. They happened only in imagination, or in books, first met in Tove Jansson's Moominland, then in the writings of the Russians on their beloved dachas – black tea on the terrace, pale green shutters, orchards and old roses. Just the phrase *Summer house for rent* was full of promise. The promise of repeated summers. The hope of pleasure still to come. *Will there be pleasure still to come?*

In Jansson's books, a summerhouse is a place apart. I look up Klovharun, her island home and by extension the other islands of the Pellinge archipelago, Bisaballen,

Langhallskobben, Kummelskar, to see how improbably small they are and how remote. A community of 250 island-dwellers, spread over 200 islands across the Gulf of Finland. On a map they leave their own distinctive mark, like a trail of breadcrumbs across a tablecloth or a white dish dropped from a height and smashed in pieces.

Jansson the island-dweller was fierce about the geography of islands, their demarcations, privations and many joys. Klovharun remains private. Landing is restricted. The map of Moominland is stark, beset on all sides by natural forces, floods and frosts and comets and volcanoes. It is a world shot through with oppositions much like ours: freedom and loneliness, community and separation, summer and winter, darkness and light. Jansson was good on boundaries, on how the protocols of the people of an island differed from the protocols of the people of the mainland, or how the long summer might be differentiated as a time apart, bracketed from the singular isolation of the even longer winter.

On an island you could prepare yourself. See a boat coming from afar and take avoiding action if you wished. A visitor, even with the best intentions, might be unwelcome and sail away disappointed, leaving a parcel of books, some fish wrapped in paper, a flashlight or a pair of new boots on the jetty. The terrible thing, worst of all as Jansson would have it, was to be stuck on an island with a person you did not like. This was not to be our fate.

My childhood summers were spent on crowded camping sites in Wales, or caravans in windswept fields with breeze-block showers and chemical toilets near at hand. The opposite of islands, and anyway, it wasn't summer. *Summer house not for rent in winter* was an anomaly and so were we. It was out of season, and we were not by any stretch, on holiday.

Holiday homes are an excursion into other people's preoccupations. Weightless but not without risk, like putting your hand into the pocket of a stranger. Maybe you'd find a piece of lint, a coin, a ticket, a ball of tissue . . . something worse. Someone's idea of home might not quite dovetail with your own. I had no expectations on arrival at Small Paynes so was not disappointed. We needed a place to be together. In times of crisis, you can't just dial the body down to zero, withdraw from heat and lie like small mammals under rock to wait it out. Perhaps that time will come in future. For now, these are the bodies we've been given. Garland, the child and me, his mother. We all have to exist somewhere.

My decision had been to say *yes* and not think too hard about it. I had not chosen Small Paynes, nor had any role in its appearance but could sense as soon as we arrived how well it fitted us. Like a second-hand coat picked out at random from a rail, which turned out to be my size, its idea of home fell loosely within the framework of my own.

At Small Paynes when we woke, the sun was already out, going about its business from first light, smashing through windows, drying off the little stones, bleaching the paint off everything it saw and flaying the house bare. Even in winter the sun did its atomic work inside and out. Wipe too hard on the kitchen table and paint came off in your hands in muted flakes of blue and green so light they floated. Chasing Garland bare-naked round the room to dry him after his bath, I watched his skin frisk off in minute layers to dance in the hanging light, all motes conjoining in the air together, mineral, animal, paint and skin, suspended in communion. Garland ran fast and reckless at all hazards: sharp corners on tables, slippery rocks, or waves that might come from nowhere in my imagination and carry him out to sea. *Is this our house?* he asked. Of course. How would it not be ours? Garland was everywhere. He filled the space and renewed himself with each new day within it. *Yes*, I said. *This is where we are.*

There was no dust. Sand is clean. Dust is unclean. That is the law, the natural state of things. The wind blew all the dust away and sand, being heavier, took its place and filled up every crevice and so, in consequence, the place seemed clean. After a few days, we too were clean as skeletons; picked over, boned and brined and watered down. Sand came in the house inside our socks and shoes, deep in our hoods, our pockets and in the hems of trousers, stripping the wooden floors and anything it came in contact with. Sand smoothed the edges off the chairs, took the skin down from our faces and papered the pebbles we brought in to sweet and gleamy ovals that sat in the palm of the hand like you could suck them. Garland's hair made comic, concrete stands and quiffs upon his head that quickly would not take a comb. We became drier, harder, more polished versions of ourselves. And when we left, the sand came with us, and fell between the floorboards back at home where it remained, like samples from another planet, forever out of reach.

There wasn't much to do outside the sea and dunes. The creek. The oyster beds. We walked the main street, bare and void of summer hustle, the whole way down and back again. In summer that trip alone could take a couple hours, they said, by the time you'd looked in all the stores and said hello to all the people. The place was rammed from May through till October. No one could get a room. In winter it was empty. A whole town full of vacancies.

We went to the library to pass one afternoon and sat on small chairs in the children's section while Garland riffled through the stacks until he found a book that suited him. *The New Encyclopaedia of the World*. Garland loves encyclopaedias. This is a visual one that runs non-alphabetically through an index beginning with *The Universe*, then in short chapters: *Prehistoric Earth. Plants. Animals. The Human Body. The Sea. Geology. Meterology. Transport. The Visual Arts. Architecture. Music. Sport*. It closed with *Everyday Things* – a section packed with all the things we think we cannot do without: toasters and shoes and clocks and drills. The computer, out of date as soon as the book was printed, and the saddle, coming directly after the lawnmower as if harnessed functionally together.

Garland was of an age to like pictures and facts and curious about the gap between them so this brought two of his favourite stimulations together, the connecting of image to word. New landforms come to his attention, like *Tombolo – an isthmus of sand or shingle that connects an island to the mainland.* This was a new one to me too and seemed somehow to encapsulate our current situation. I imagined us picking our way carefully along a fragile strip as if our lives depended on it, the sea fretting at our feet from either side.

Chapter Six. *Coastlines are among the most rapidly changing landscape features.* I'll take change over permanence any day. If anyone had asked me, that's what I would have said, but that was before change took us and shook us inside out. At the edge, things fray. At the edge there is only uncertainty.

We had packed no books for the journey. Books, like the stones we brought in from the beach, were too heavy for the plane, and even the thought of reading too strenuous an encounter. The word was raw upon the page. In the last year, kindly, and with the best intentions, a stack of books had come our way to illustrate the concept of dying. These books were mainly aimed at Garland, yet adults are as much novices as children in this regard.

In children's books about the dead, the living and the dying both are often represented at one remove as animals. Badgers and birds and mice and voles and elephants: all have their sorrows and their natural endings. *Why are they all lions?* asked Garland carefully, stopped at a page with Granny lion declining under a duvet in a suburban bedroom, framed by her handsome family, son Simba, daughter-in-law Nuala, cubs, and close members of the pride. In another book, the dead were drawn as dinosaurs with bright white teeth and smiling faces. I flicked right through. Dead. All dead. Extinct and gone. A meteorite did for the dinosaurs in a rain of sulphurous rock to make a toxic mausoleum that spanned the globe for years. The dinosaurs died in hell. Their earth their tomb.

Some books took a metaphysical route. The individual soul shown as a single raindrop falling into the sea, at once a droplet singular and precious, yet indivisible within the whole. This is a tricky one to think and harder still to draw. The scene was loosely scribbled in pale colours that bled over the white page like an ocean of crayon tears across a double spread. It was an image without end. From the kitchen at Small Paynes, where the sea's volume banked outside the window on a daily basis, the sea was an unspeakable thing of darkness without a pastel to be seen. Entire taxonomies of tone collapsed under its weight. The single drop of water all alone, under colossal pressure, almighty depth and stupendous cold, was a vision of annihilation. It made you want to cry. The sea was a black hole for colour. The sea was where colour went to die.

I did not rate these illustrations, nor did I rate the questions raised. *How do bees die?* asked Garland, abandoning the lions-in-mourning to lightly run cars in loops across the floor.

Bees die alone, I said – too rough – and just as quick, regretted it. We left the books back home.

We spent the days with Dina and Maeve, but the nights and early mornings were ours. Mornings made surplus, extra time that seemed to stack outside the usual hours and pass therefore more slowly. Mornings, we had a single plan and stuck to it. Hats, coats and scarves. Onto the beach. Stay out as long as we could bear.

Night was a different proposition. Dusk signalled a shift in register of all material things. Things that were soft by day, turned solid, and things that were open, folded shut. Dusk was the cue. The feeling strengthened as the light slacked off. The house, porous by day and shot through from many angles by the sun, sealed itself in. The building tightened and pulled its timbers round. The kitchen lamp made inroads against the dark. Glass silvered over. Reflections massed and gathered strength. The kitchen was doubled into being in the window, summoned and rendered clearer by the minute, by the second, until in a final flourish, the battle with the dark was won.

Each night it was the same. The window became a mirror. The room reflected back, a picture. The house became an island. Everything else had gone. The sea gone too, collapsed in darkness. Black like the backstage black of a theatre after the lights go out. You could only guess the sea from its proximity and what you knew of it already – a vast intelligence in its lair, gathering its strength by moonlight, communicating ceaselessly with other seas worldwide. The strip of beach, so broad and generous by day, was relegated to a narrow, inky apron, void of all yellow. Beyond that point we did not go.

Those early nights in the kitchen at Small Paynes were

solo, rehearsals for the first of many. *Will I get used to this?* For Garland, home was where we were together. That it was not our house he did not mind. A child is pretext for many female roles. By day I cared for him, fed him and sang to him, hugged him and bathed him, but in the kitchen late at night, with him asleep, my cover broke. I was alone, and like an extra in a play, pushed forward unexpectedly to narrate my lines in front of an audience I could not see, I came unstuck. I did not know my part. How should I speak? No voice came and no ideas, not then, and not for a long time after. The face reflected back, made ghoulish by the kitchen lamp, was mine, but its expression? That was unreadable, even to me. To be pictured in the window at Small Paynes was to be projected outwards over the sea like a magic lantern. After I went to bed, I had the sense that my reflection lingered and remained there till daybreak as a warning visible only to ships. A figurehead, a phantom, glowing green-blue phosphor against the glass.

I am not one for dreaming, not now, not then or ever, but that first night at Small Paynes Landing, I dreamt that someone called out Garland's name and woke him and he in turn woke me. He did wake me, that bit was real, but in the glassy stages of the first minutes, I worried about who had called to him. It could not have been his father, but it was such a vivid cry from a third person, I thought I must have dreamt the friend who slept in the spare room at home the night before we left, and in my dream, made him a stand-in for the trio we once were. Though I was disappointed on waking to find there were still just two of us, there was something reassuring in such a brisk game of wake-up tag. It meant that we were in some truncated fashion, the two of us, still viable and still a unit. It was only a dream, but dreams call to events in life. It felt familiar.

68

9

It is useful in moments of distress to be occupied with that which is in front of you. That's what they said at home. Work can be good in this regard, the heavy lifting work that fills up space but also the small-scale, distracting stuff that packs between. Routines, they said: sorting, tidying, putting things away, shifting around and making good. The trick it seemed was to find a groove that held you safe and let you shuttle forward, even for a short time, then slowly, expand your groove until it seemed wide enough to approximate a life – or something else happened to derail you, whichever was the sooner. I could do that. In this respect, on the beach at Small Paynes, Garland and I were scientists in pursuit of the empirical. We had the time and little else to do. The beach was our laboratory.

The wind put paid to thinking. The wind was horizontal, too strong for speech, so most days we were mute. If you opened your mouth, sand flew in. The best way to beat the wind was keep our heads down, hoods on and hunt for pebbles and shells. The stones were the colour of biscuits flashed in the sun and sprung from a central furnace: churned a million times, fired a million times. We sifted stones like workers on an hourly rate, picked them up and dropped them, stashed them in our pockets or hurled them into the water. Neither of us could throw. There were no skimmers on that stretch. The stones were small and various but generally round or flat, and smooth as beads. The sea did its work well.

With pebbles of surpassing beauty, we showed them to each other for mutual acclaim and the ones we admired, we swapped to be doubly admired. Like jewels in the catalogue of an auctioneer, turning the pages slowly, we were amazed, and felt for each in turn a huge pull in the moment of first settling in the hand. *This one! No, this one!* As if such things had not been seen before and would not come again.

Chopped granite, bevelled edge, small blemishes.
'Licked' stone, with diametric transverse markings. Milky
A duck-shaped rock, green as bile. Adamantine

To pick up a stone was to demarcate it from the others, yet to describe a single stone in words was like trying to describe the narrowing of an eye – doomed to failure. To make a choice of one thing over another opens a space that focuses attention. Ideas are given room: concepts of beauty, texture, weight and speed and memory and time, are all presented for comparison. Culture is always made in context. It is communal and does not happen in a vacuum. Ours was a handmade culture, not based in language, but culture none the less. We rubbed each pebble smoothness between finger and thumb in mutual admiration, turning them over and over like a puzzle that might be understood if only we had some crucial, missing, metaplasmic key. The gap between a thing in the hand and an idea in the head is vast and volatile. *Stone* becomes *tone* becomes *one* becomes *on* becomes, over time, a smooth and flattened *o*.

Basalt: extraneous, igneous, made from cooling lava, can form columns as lava cools and surfaces contract. Hard.

Slate: forms close to the surface under pressure and temperature. Pressure causes clay minerals to line up in parallel. Splits easily into sheets. Soft.

In the lives of rocks, the temptation is to think of geologic time as in the past and of geology as history, with its early, tectonic phase of crashing continents, reducible to a lurid graphic, over and done. This is clearly not the case, the evidence is visible around us, but lives, as we know, are short. Short-termism is not the only problem humans face but it's a big one. It may yet be our undoing.

The sea is a master-mason. Maker. Un-maker. Even when calm, it is deceptive. The sea can spin a brutal shard into a docile pebble over a long arc. A piece of sandstone the size of a Sherbet Orange is sucked clean in the sea's mouth long before it takes a bite from a chunk of granite. New stones are forming all the time. A slab of rock splits from a cliff and falls onto the beach below. The fragment softens, blurs, then over time abrades, returning sight unseen, to grain. The sea worries at the land's soft belly and the land surrenders, folds, or holds, according to its nature. Change is the constant. Everything else is incidental.

Thinking of those mornings on the beach at Small Paynes, it was the feel of Garland's hand in mine that I remember and the particularity of each stone that passed between us that made each moment in its own way special, yet afterwards, I knew that we would not recall the colour and feel of any pebble beyond the event of its finding, and all the moments of finding, taken together, would not add up to anything like the sum of hours spent looking. It was an activity of great intensity that served no clear purpose, except to anchor us in place and time and to each other. We were assembling an inventory of small exchanges, ephemeral but no less actual. *Look what I found!* A succession of present moments with each shared stone unique, a mark of reassurance, a sign of life. *A smooth ovoid, the colour of garnet, shot through with veins of pink . . .*

Back in the kitchen, the moment fell away. Now we were done collecting. To pull the glass door shut dialled down the wind and cut the sea's noise in half. The finds slipped back to pebbles. Garland piled them on the floor to pass as landscape for his dinosaurs to roam. Forms can slip. We knew first-hand how slippery forms could be. An object could skip from thing to word and back again, from solid, to nothing at all. A person might just vanish. It happens all the time. If Garland dropped his favourite stone at any moment – very likely – *a pressed, near-perfect egg, jet black when wet* – onto the beach and walked three paces more, he would not find it and just as quick forget it. What would he remember of Small Paynes? And Sam? His father. What would he know of him?

Unlike jewels, the stones we valued would not travel, nor did they keep their worth. They had no legacy. When it was time to go, we piled them up outside the door and left them. With the transaction over, the stones had become weight. Garland was a scavenger of some commitment. He made a plaintive case to take them home, but it was weak. He knew when he was beaten. We came with so much baggage already.

Stones showed the way to water, sticks, to land. If I am sentimental about anything in Garland's early childhood, it is for the charismatic sticks and magic stones of no account brought home. Toys came and went, they broke, got lost, were handed on, but these were the tokens of an expanding occult world.

Garland's room had fast become a depository for finds of no particular distinction. He had three shelves, one books, another, pebbles, gathered from beaches within a day's radius. A small, adjoining shelf held cacti. They looked quite dead – maybe they were. The stones, the cacti and the books were soft with dust. Once allowed entry, we let things lie.

Children are anthropologists and this is fieldwork. To find things, pick them up and carry them, these are the means by which they understand the world. Garland took this seriously. He was a collector. Babies will draw the world by stem or stone into their mouths. The visual leaves them wanting more. After they learn how not to eat the things they see, they cling to them, even while scouting wild-eyed for the next find. It is the choosing that is of interest and the power therefore invested in the object by being picked. The thing, such as it is, is secondary. Under Garland's bed were hauls of sticks of varying lengths, one weaponised to points at either end, the rest would do no harm at all: a rudimentary spoon that more resembled a club. A branch shaped very like a Y. Twin vines, coiled hard and dry around each other and now inseparable.

Once home, their status as trophies disappeared but they clung on. Sticks had the shorter span – they got thrown out eventually – but stones, even the most unpromising, remained, and once inside, by process of inertia, they were beached. *Deposition occurs when the forces responsible for sediment transportation are no longer sufficient to overcome the forces of gravity and friction, creating a resistance to motion; this is known as the null-point hypothesis.* This was the point Garland was at.

A flat flint nibbled down one edge. A pebble scored with harsh, blue, woad-like markings. A white hag stone shaped like a goddess bored straight through. A piece of glass, moulded to sweetness by a river. Stones may be deep time but for all that, he hardly looked at them again. The objects acquired a second life by deposition in our home, unseen but contributing in tiny ways as debris, piled on the floor of our existence. For Garland, the explorer, the gap between outside – nature – and inside – home – was porous and infinitely negotiable. Objects of significance moved freely between these worlds.

I O

How do we learn? By repetition. On a beach, I bounce Garland into the low waves. Digging holes is the first thing he wants to do, and after that, this is the next thing. His fat legs paw the waves to kick them off. He is not one metre high. *Where is she taking me?* For a child, the sea is a wall immediately upon them, ready to collapse at any moment. Excitement curdles into fear. *Why is she laughing?* The tide is a game, and its rules are clear until you get them wrong and then you are upended in a slap of salt, to be plucked by someone, who could be anyone and not your mother, from the edge, or in the worst case – not to be considered here – taken.

As classified by the Smithsonian, the ring-tailed lemur has a range of facial expressions correlating with its need to communicate. These include:

- Staring, open-mouth face
- Staring, bared-teeth scream face

- Silent, bared-teeth face
- Pout face
- Hoot face

As an infant, Garland the animal did all these, adding to his repertoire only three crucial human emotives: smiling face, laughing face, collapsing tears face.

It was a puzzle sometimes what there was to say. I was the adult, but unsure where his needs ended and mine began. We sat across the table from each other in the kitchen. The sun on a dagger slant between us. Eggs, juice, coffee, pieces of apple browning in a bowl . . . *Children must eat fruit. Why won't he eat more fruit?* It was not Garland's job to make me feel less lonely, yet at Small Paynes he could chase my spirits higher in an instant: light and simple, as a balloon inflates with air. Who needed who more? I wouldn't have come without him. But now that we were here – what were we even doing?

One morning on the beach as usual, I saw a man on the horizon. This was an unfamiliar sight and, stranger still, the man was walking on the water. That would be rare at any hour. I am open to the mysterious but stop short of miracles. Could be that grief had done its demolition work. Or maybe the fireball sun had fused the synapses that linked image to understanding and this was the first of many apparitions come to haunt me and I should just get used to them. As he approached, the mystery cleared. I could see how he advanced in waders up to his waist, a man quite certain of his place on earth, tracking the curve of the bay with giant steps, like Atlas keeping in shape for the job of holding up the sky. A fisherman by the leathered look of him I guessed. *Hello.* He did not slow down or speak and seemed surprised, not pleased, to see us.

No human as far as anyone could see within the curve of the visible world but nor would he break his stride to acknowledge us, a woman and child out on the sand in the early hours. Exposed under this scrutiny, I was a mad mother. I imagined the conversation later in the bar.

What was that lady doing with a kid out there? Nuts!

At night, when Garland slept, the question grew in form and took on shadow shapes. To better examine it, I lay on the floor to study the ceiling – a whitewashed hardboard, pinned in place with battens, it held my attention for hours. I lay on the couch and took in the wall. I lay on the mat and took in the corner. I lay on the bed and took in the window and beyond that, the sea. Viewed from land, the sea is impenetrable.

At night, I understood that it was Garland's presence as physical force that kept me standing. Without him I might lie down and not get up. Grief is fatigue. Going limp is a known resistance strategy. As passive protest, it is effective. *Let someone else take care of you . . . carry you off.* At night, the building's basic structure, such as it was, a plain ceiling, doors and lintels, windows, floor, was underpinned by two distinctive sounds, one flat, one upright, overlapping: the sea shushing the stones, and Garland's breathing, rising and falling, under or over the sound of waves it was hard to tell. At Small Paynes the sea would never keep its distance. It slipped into our dreams and held us under but even there, I noticed Garland's breathing, ever-present, steady, keeping time. Garland's breathing was that of a champion sleeper, victorious in all conditions short-term and long.

Loneliness is not having no one to talk to. You can be in the thick of the crowd, a glass in your hand, the life and very soul, and still be lonely. Loneliness is not finding the talk you want to talk. Being compelled to talk another's talk. That is the worst. The world is reflected back to us in speech. If you say the words you want to say and there is no adequate response – it is better to remain silent. Children learn this early and respond accordingly. The talk I wished to talk, the one I knew the rhythms of by heart, was gone. In its absence, there were various formal configurations:

- Talking and being heard
- Talking and not being heard
- Talking to keep yourself company
- Talking to keep others company
- Talking to keep others at bay
- Vocalising
- Laughing
- Shouting
- Screaming
- Bawling

Silent, bared-teeth face. That would have to do.

A child does not hold what you say or refract it back. That's not their role. A child's talk comes in volleys. It can be a fun game for the duration, but one player is less than competent and cannot catch, hit, or run with the ball. If I had been asked to describe what we spoke about in that time at Small Paynes, I would have been blank. Whatever sense we made was fixed in my remembering to the form of the wooden house, the line of the horizon and the wind that chased the sand in parallel along.

We were two figures seen from above, and therefore in context, small. If you had asked me what we did at Small

Paynes, I might have said, cautiously, after a pause, *we cared for other each in our fashion* and that would have been as accurate a response as I could make it.

In a book, when triggered by some setback or disaster, a character might go on a journey. This is a handy plot device. A second-born prince could find himself banished and set off for another kingdom far away. A princess disguises herself as a man and rides off to war for seven years. A servant girl walks miles to the sea to choose the radical life of a mermaid. Leaving does not always present an option to return. Sometimes leaving is just leaving and not being seen again. That's it. *Farewell.*

A story, any kind of story, gives us a line to take, even if only the one we tell ourselves to set us daily on the road. It is a work in progress. We craft our language in the telling to hold to the path of our experience and alter and redraft it over time. We choose the words that work for us at any point and may well choose differently next time we speak. Words that are harsh or too hysterical are dropped. People shrink from them, therefore from us. We cannot have this. Connection is the point of stories. Likewise, we discard the ones that don't quite work, too slack to hold the thing we want to say. Much is made up or misremembered. Much gets forgotten. Memory is fiction by accretion, inherently unstable and up for grabs. Language recasts itself. We replace a word that once we thought did well enough with one that takes a different slant and before you know it, you are somewhere else entirely. This is what stories do. Start off somewhere – and end up in a different place.

In the aftermath of disaster, we had fallen out of a story. We travelled to a finger of land curving into the sea in an attempt to create a new one, about two people, a mother and child. Consensus was, this was a good thing. *Go* they had all said, *Go!* As if experience might be laid down in an old set of rooms like a new carpet to make a place more liveable. But as to the nature of the story, what kind it was, or how it would end? That was unclear. Each telling failed to hit the mark. For Garland it was a hiatus, a break that followed from an ending, but not a beginning. Garland had only been alive a short while. He was still at the start of his beginning. You cannot keep on beginning. At a certain point you just have to get on with it. Where did that leave me?

Widowed.

Huh.

When you are a single person with a child, there will be those who think you have been left. I thought at first it was something in my face, a quality of dislocation. *L'abandonata* – the woman left behind. There is a special sorrow in store for the abandoned. Pity, fear. All the pale laundry neatly folded.

He would never have left me. He just died. Usually, I think this, but once, by mistake, said it out loud in the garden of a country pub. I could wish for a better setting, but you do not get to choose your moments. It was at one of those outside tables that are hard to get your legs beneath, with people who were not my friends, but friends of the friends who introduced us and therefore to me, nobodies. Six of those people at one table is five too many. I remember the knot of legs under the table, but not their faces. Considering the amount of death there is in the world, we are often still surprised to hear about it.

A half-pint of bitter please . . .

Salt and vinegar please . . .

Thank you.

At the time I had not quite believed them, those advocates

of going away, but had gone along with it. When people gave advice, I took it. The line of least resistance is still a line. Something to hold to. There hadn't been an option marked *Do nothing*. Garland did not present a *Do nothing* option.

We cared for each other in our fashion. Childcare for a single parent is a single channel. It is a gutter, a fixed seam, down which the world flushes each day while you watch it pass without the energy to more than mark its passing. As an activity it is inarticulate. Hard to write down. Hard to recall in retrospect. The beach at Small Paynes was circular time, an ancient sinkhole with its own vortex into which mothers could wish time itself away. There were of course no other mothers, no other children, and Garland the tyrant, dragged me onto it each morning to do the wishing and the sinking. To an outside observer – it was February, there were no observers – I was a model parent, proving her worth time and again. Ever attentive, in countless ways I showed my love. See how I fussed with his scarf, sand in his eyes, sunscreen, stones in the shoe, all the small yet necessary things that fill the days spent looking after children, while being at the same time absent, so far estranged I feared I might not notice him even while fixing his scarf for the umpteenth time or buttoning his coat against the wind. But thinking back, maybe it was only the fixing and buttoning that held me in place, so lightly tethered. Here was the job in hand. I was a caretaker mother while waiting for the time of caretaker mothering to pass and willing it on, with the idea – or more, the hope – that this time would be replaced by some other kind of time that made more sense, and I might notice the difference when that happened as a structural shift, a change in mood, a crack in the pattern of what was possible. *And if it didn't?*

Yet I could see that while I was eking out existence from a nominal supply – sand, sunscreen, tiny stones – Garland was having something – implausible, but visibly the case – that might constitute *a good time*. There he was in the middle distance, dressed like a flag of my invention, blue coat, green scarf, red hat, digging up sand like a little dog and spooning it carefully onto another pile. Now he banks up the mound and wets it, smooths it down, arranges stones around the heap to make it fat. He knows exactly what to do. He is focused on his work. He does not need to turn to me. It was just an everyday task, self-devised and pleasure-giving. Garland, unfurling at a distance. It seemed like a good time. It looked like a good time. Maybe it was . . .

The north end of the beach, where the sand drifted into dunes, was where Garland liked to play hide and seek. This was a serious game for us, and fraught with risk. What if we lose each other? *What happens then?*

A little hotness in the palm makes Garland's hand go slack and he cuts loose. He's off. His footsteps fill with sand so that his tracks become invisible, to leave no trace as if erased by magic slate. You see him now. Next moment, you will not. We play this game a lot. Each step slips backward twice its length, but he persists by sheer will forward into the wind. Laughter evaporates behind him. Sand pops like salt rock candy crystal in his mouth. His daft milk teeth are pearls on a tiny string. A dune is a mountain shot through a trillion times with quartz. A child can vanish into its radiance.

Quickly he's gone, and I skid down the runnels and slides in his wake, holding to the cascades made by dogs and long-gone walkers, hard by the brackish gorse that grows rough and draws moisture from where I don't know and how deep down. Gorse in these dunes is more like rock than plant. It fuses in rudimentary shapes that flower for half the year, then nothing. Hostile to humans, it is a live artillery of spines yet teems with bugs and beetles and for the little coloured pecking birds, it is a regular metropolis. *Ready or not* I shout.

A plastic bag snagged on a thorn is the same shade as Garland's coat but is not Garland. *Who am I without him?* I *was* someone, not so long ago, before he came. Before that, someone else again. We all have many lives. Garland will too. A sunspot blooms in my eye. I turn my head. For a single, fluorescent moment, I think to run away and not look back. The thought remains there, light as a float, still sealed like an unopened capsule when we leave.

II

A discrepancy between the seen position and the felt position.
That sentence could explain much of us most of the time.
The gap between how we feel and how we are perceived. The
difference between experiencing a landscape and being seen
against it, or worse, not being seen, invisible even within it.
*The Restless Image: a discrepancy between the seen position and
the felt position* is a photograph by Rose Finn-Kelcey in which
she is pictured upside down doing a handstand on a beach,
an action that people – most often children – like to do on
beaches when the mood takes them. The horizon sets the
stage for her experience. A plain band shimmering, somewhere on the English coastline in the mid-1970s. The tide
is out.

It might be spontaneous, this action, but you know it
isn't. She's too upright, too isolate, much like a flag with
her big skirt, a standard-bearer out on her own against the
horizon, flipped in the glare of the sea light. She crosses the

confederates of land, sea, and sky. Cuts through them all like scissors. She seems taller this way than she would the right way up. Straight as a stick of rock.

Rose Finn-Kelcey liked flags. She made several works with them in public places. A giant banner with the slogan *Power for the People* was commissioned by the Central Electricity Generating Board to hang from Battersea Power Station. It didn't last long, twenty-four hours, before it was removed after objections from local residents, alarmed at such a big idea expressed so publicly. *The Restless Image* is a staged photo and in another way ephemeral. From a contact sheet with multiple takes, this is the one. She cannot hold that pose for long.

We're drawn to images of abandon. The world turned upside down. They signal slippage of the usual rules, or remind us of the bendy, flexy bodies we once had as children and the dignity we didn't have back then to lose. We showed our knickers and didn't mind. *Carefree*, as we imagine in our heads. When she made the piece, Finn-Kelcey was thinking of a photo of her mother playing on a beach as a child. The discrepancy between her mother as a child, and her mother as her mother, between being someone yourself, and being someone to someone else.

A second, solitary figure walks the sands. A man. He is the right way up and so, like us, a representative of the natural order but he is tiny, too far away to be a party to the action. The camera is her witness and so are we. Her skirt flares like an iridescent shell, some sort of mollusc, elegantly fluted and her shape is a tern diving into water. How to communicate how we feel to others? How to communicate anything at all? That is the task in hand. It's hard. Blood to the head. The world spins. The sky falls below the horizon. The earth swoops up to take its place.

*

This is our last week at Small Paynes Landing. A few days more and we'll be going home. Dina has arranged a massage as a parting gift, and I say yes though it seems an unlikely prospect. We may have crossed the ocean, but my body is another country altogether. Dimly I understand the concept – that a massage might connect a vagrant brain to its housing. The masseuse is called Kay or Joy or maybe K-Joy or maybe nothing like that at all, but it's a small community and everyone here knows her and smiles to hear her name. Her place is a trailer set in piney woods at the edge of town. Putting together the idea of outlying woods and isolated trailer, I make a standard composite, an outcast crone with leathered skin: shorthand – a witch, but K-Joy is younger than me and her skin is the skin of a person who has a full life and lives on the right mix of foods for her metabolism: fish, nuts, and vegetables. Her face is round as an O. I have a moonlike face and I am drawn to other moonish faces, but hers is fuller. Her hair is buzz-cut short – Carl Dreyer's Joan of Arc with way more sun – and her eyes are clear with the whites of them especially white in the style of of American teeth. My whites are yellow and my eyes dry with sand and the winter sun that stays low. Of the two of us, I am the crone, no contest.

K-Joy lives at a point where the houses stop, the beach runs off into the woods and then, with little demarcation, ends. There's a short zone of scattered cones and twigs on sandy ground with sparse, dry growth that pokes through here and there, and then you are in the woods proper where spindly trees cut the sun's rays down to slivers before they reach bare earth. Dina takes Garland off to play. Running through trees, he's sliced into dark and lighter beams that blend with the trunks. Quickly they vanish into a mix of shade and pattern.

I tell K-Joy I am in no way ready to be touched and I am being flippant to start up conversation but also not. I remember that touch has power, but the thought has been wilfully arrested. It is blocked. She laughs. She knows how people can lose connection with their bodies, roam unharnessed, sometimes never to return. Her job is to hold them, reassure them, guide them gently back within their frame. In this respect alone, if in no other, she is a witch. *Sure, I'll go easy* she says.

Of all the senses, four are readily located; eyes, nose, ears, mouth, but the last is more mysterious and everywhere at home. We are sensual all along our length and touch is the pressure of the world against our limits. We gauge in turn our impact on it. It is a primary response, innate, that grows in parallel with our inception and we are forever hungry for its information. A newborn will turn its head towards the slightest stroke. A hand, unwanted, on a knee, is understood immediately as code. A game of tag drives children mad to be the first to lay a finger on each other. The world without touch is hardest to imagine.

The woman in the photo upside down holds up the world. Damp sand shifts under her hands. It gives her the intelligence she needs. Palms splayed, she steadies, stabilises, keeps to centre. Her fingers know the score. This is the felt position. Touch without context is nothing – yet here I am so far from home, so careless, so unthinking even, saying yes to a stranger.

The trailer is parked on blocks and framed by a set of wooden steps all hung with shells. The town is garlanded with shells, as if pledging allegiance in perpetuity to the sea. If shells were currency, they would all be rich. The place is warm in winter sun. Blankets and hanging fabrics distract the eye and divide the small space into sections. They do it well. The box on wheels becomes a maze of colour and pattern that make up diversions and new sightlines. The kitchen is one step up, another down to a treatment area with the massage bed tucked under the window facing the trees, so that the light that falls there is always shaded, indirect and filtered through pines. Behind a printed hanging, there is a space that might be a tiny bedroom and a small sitting area is visible through a free-standing shelf that doubles as a screen. A mirror, partly obscured by a thick hand-painted rainbow, sits on a ledge beside the massage table, next to a row of crystals neatly in a line. They are pale and not at all dusty. A grey-green plant has fuzz around the scissored cut-out edges of each leaf that looks like fur and on inspection, it is not dusty either. I expect to see cat hairs but there are none. This is the second thing about which I am wrong. The place is very clean.

I'd like to look round but as much as K-Joy is a free spirit, she is a professional, so quickly I lie down, legs under a folded orange blanket. She has warmed the blanket on a heater. In turn I warm to her. Pressing my cheek against the bed, the layer of needles under pines reads from a distance as brown snow, blurring the contours of the land. The beach must be not so far beyond, but the trees and fallen cones muffle the sea so you can't hear it. Pines deaden all noise. No one can see us here in the woods. We are at the outer limit of the town, on a spit of land at the edge of the sea, and she is about to start.

The components of the scene are set. A blanket – orange, warm. A house on wheels. The sea – close by. Garland – elsewhere. Duration – one hour. I think I'm ready. I make a mental note to go along with it, whatever comes, annihilation – and its aftermath. I've no idea. To be worked on down to nothing would be a blessing, but what rises conversely, and unforeseen, is a stubborn wish to be left alone. Whatever my position is, it is the one I take. I'm in my fastness. This is the place I feel secure. I said yes to K-Joy and a massage because I say yes now as default to things. I say yes because there is an impetus to *yes* that *no* does not possess, and impetus has force behind it that might lead somewhere. But yes, in my mouth is an uncertain thing. It is brittle. Saying *yes*, I hadn't thought it through. I had not understood in fact the fundamental thing. A massage would involve *touch*. This is a simple failure of the imagination. Someone would touch me. I was going to feel something. When I said yes, I meant no but it is now too late. This is the third thing about which I am wrong.

In the glacial time that followed after he died, months, or maybe years perhaps, how long it was I cannot tell, I did not want a lover. Men's bodies crumpled in the wrong way. Their breath came from a place to be resisted. Words fell from their mouths like stones to become part of a pre-existing landscape indistinguishable from what was there before. To be with them, was to view them through a long lens. It was a distance I could not hope to cover and if they could even see me back, I was not sure. Love is change. *That's good!* they said. But love is also hungry. It makes demands. Takes energy. Of that I had little and such that I had, I hoarded. This was no time for expansion.

Garland's hugs are loose. They happen on the fly. Self-absorption stakes out the limits of his holding and he is readily distracted, as if I am merely one item in his expanding repertoire and there is always something or someone else for him to lay a hand upon. His touch is known, his growing weight familiar. But here *she* is. This person Kay or Joy. A stranger, strangely welcomed in. Her fingers are on my skin. She places her palms together on my back and smooths them apart as if flattening a set of wings the better to admire them. She presses gently onto the fibres of my neck and keeps on pressing, lightly skilful, down between the layers and further still to find a certain seam she knows is there. She rolls her hands out from the high and complex middle range to the outer shelves of my terrain while meeting no resistance. I stand no chance. I am defenceless. The sea rolls in. It only takes a minute. Pulls me under. Yes, and also, no. My cheek, pressed to the mat is wet and hot. We are not four minutes in. The wind is up. The pines begin to rock.

Afterwards she makes me a tisane of pale leaves and we sit in the pale sun on the pale step to wait for the others to return. The cup shakes in my hand and the tea picks up the tremor, as if its job is simply to record the pattern and play it back for me to see. I am a person of paper, light and insubstantial. We talk about nothing, continuing to sit. The cup is in my hand. The tea is in the cup. I drink it. Slowly the cycle stills.

Looking for photos from Small Paynes Landing some years on, I was surprised to find four. I take so many pictures all the time. The place remained imprinted in my head: sand, sea, horizon, pressed out in such distinctive bands that I was sure the memory would be backed by a vast companion set of images which I could later scroll through and share with Garland after enough time had passed, but there were four. All were of Garland on the beach. In each he is absorbed. He does not see the camera. In one he walks away from me. A small diminishing figure, he follows the line of the sea.

Rose Finn-Kelcey
The Restless Image: a discrepancy
between the seen position
and the felt position (1975)
Photograph, gelatin silver print
on paper mounted on board
664 × 1014 mm

HOME

12

Where does loss live?

This is not a philosophical question. It is physical. Loss has no lexicon, yet it is everywhere unnamed. Silt builds in sedimentary layers over time to raise new ground. Losses mount to become simply experience. A scar forms tissue over the site of a wound. The skin will never be as supple again. To grow older is to add to the pile of things available to lose, a discard pile of things you loved or places you used to feel at home, of people who have stopped, and do not now continue.

I did not need to teach any of this to Garland. I could see that Garland was hard at work sorting it out for himself. Children are natural improvisers. They build the world of their imagination, make huts from sticks and leaves, divert rivers, dam streams with mud. To understand the world, they use the things that are to hand.

You know what we could do? We could take an Asimo and cover it with Dad stuff, sort of like make it a skin of Dad's things.

This was a Tuesday morning. Now we were one year into a routine of sorts. It was a holding pattern. *It is useful in moments of distress to be occupied with that which is in front of you . . .* That's what they said. I had gone back to work and Garland started school. My mind was on the meeting ahead and the skirt I was wearing. Yellow stripes. I knew it was the wrong skirt but could not think what the right one would be for such a meeting.

Don't make me sad!

Why is that sad?

What is that thing anyway?

What thing?

An Asimov.

An Ah-Zim-Oh.

What is that?

A robot. It's a robot that is able to climb stairs and run and stuff. It's from Japan.

That's crazy! Dad would have done anything to avoid running. Dad would be reading a book. How would Ah-Zim-Oh read a book? (I did not say out loud of course – but thought it, *Where is Ah-Zim-Oh's brain?*) *Where did you learn about Ah-Zim-Oh anyway?*

We saw a video at school.

Good try boy. Good try. Well worth a shot.

When someone dies, you lose what they meant to you. The loss is echoed in those close by like a shout bouncing off a hard surface. There is no give. Friends gather round like people jammed into a lift. They have the best intentions, but they do not absorb.

Loss is singular and plural, one and many. There is the loss of the physical self, the one you took in your arms, and its numerous, absent and in-attendant, stand-in selves – emotional, comical, creative, practical, lumpen, annoying, space-taking, surprising, delightful – each a substitute or marker for the person that once was. And then there is the inverse, the shape that's left behind, like the backwash of a wave that scoops out shingle in its wake. *You lose what you meant to them.* This is the self, reflected back.

The dead mean something to the living, that we know and that we mourn. We eulogise, write books, commission headstones and monuments, name new buildings and rename existing ones, in an attempt to do homage to those who are no longer here. But think how much the living meant to the dead! There is no monument to that. The vastness of it. How much the dead adored the living in their turn. It is a permanent conundrum. As well as losing the one they love, the clearly, not-so-immutable object, the still-living lose the state of *being-loved*. This is not passive, nor a lesser state. *Being-loved* is active, it is addictive, high and daily dopamine. Big Pharma. Its side effects are legion. It should be available on prescription were that possible to arrange.

In the aftermath of his father's death, Garland's body was like a diagram in Chinese medicine. Face down on the bed of the acupuncturist where I went on a weekly basis in those early months for reasons I could not name, I had a lot of time to study the skinny aloe vera on the shelf and pinned above it, slightly askew, the laminated chart of the annotated therapeutic subject, half man-half diagram, embellished with all a chart's creative licence and flair. Meridians ran like deltas through the body. Points seeded like stars across the whole. Eyes. Bladder. Belly. Knees. Skin. Nose. Toes. These are the sites of understanding. Eyes hurt. Bladder hurts. Belly hurts. Knees hurt. Skin hurts. Nose hurts. Toes hurt. It all hurts.

The body always calls the tune. Cell by cell and note by note. The brain doesn't know the tune so it must follow, poorly at first but then in time, more fluently as it goes, it learns the tune by heart.

Face down on the bed of the acupuncturist I had time to pay attention to the body as a map, a land spread out. Not my own. I wasn't thinking of my own body. Though prostrate and for the duration of the session, physically present, in truth I was not really there. My mind was fixed on Garland. Garland's body. How was loss moving in him? Where did it hurt? How might I ease its path?

Loss is material. We are creatures of liquid, fluids, salts: *half water*, as doctors like to say. Adults are sixty per cent solution and infants more liquid still, conduits of rapt, emotive passages scrolled tight as the inner ear. The womb is a water world from which we emerge in search of air. Information is waterborne, to be carried as pain, as tic, as glitch, as spasm through the body. This is where loss lives. Sudden shocks can flood the system: block, dam, surge, submerge. Grief can exist as a primary physical mode that seeks attention – we kick and scream, shout out, collapse, resist – or take effect more subtly over time as a rolling, evolving train of consequences. Blinking. Sniffing. Scratching. Coughing. Hurting. Ever mobile. Let me count the ways.

One mode takes hold. The child is consumed. *Monster!* It will pass. Then another will appear in its place, and you regret the loss of the one that so upset you yesterday. You swiftly miss the old ways, though the old ways lasted no time at all. Each phase is short as a bat in flight, and just as hard to track, yet seems to last forever. Sometimes I would see a tic transforming overnight as grief moped round the body, like a woman trying on different coats, *the long, the blue, the black, the dark, the check, the fur*, to find the one best-fitting. Grief is skilled in guises. It was relief the child was looking for. Who would not want relief? Grief was looking for an exit. She was working herself out.

It's sometimes hard to see what is in front of you, still less to understand it. Mostly I stood too close, but sometimes, as a strategist overlooks a battle, I could see where a skirmish might go next and try to head it off. For sure it was a war zone. The fight was physical, fast-moving, and destructive.

Blinking was the first action. In May of that first slow-moving year, Garland started blinking. Blink is too light a word, too thin, too blank. A blink is fleet as a dragonfly beat, swift and easily missed. This was a sudden shuttering that signalled the collapse of the whole apparatus. *What is the word for this?* Each blink-so-called was an action in slow motion that took its toll upon his face, jamming eyes, nose, cheeks, forehead, *down*, like an eccentric blind in a little shop or a garage door that could no longer be relied upon to stay inside its wayward runners. Metal sheared from metal. Gears crashed out of lock. His psyche went down and the whole face went down with it. Evenings, when he was tired, were worse. On the sofa watching television, his brain screwed up his face despite his best attempts to claim it back. Garland *blinking* seemed only describable in the present. To see it, you could not imagine it stopping, but in its absence, such disfigurement was unimaginable. Now we were five months in.

My first response was not to look – and then I wouldn't see him hurting. This is not a long-term strategy. Once you get used to them, tics are simply the way a person bundles; a repertoire of muscular fireworks that register as parts of an interconnected whole, along with hair colour, dark rings under the eyes, or certain habits of voice. As one *blink* crashed in against another, wave on wave, I was still trying to affect for both of us a miracle of escape. Blinking was a sign that I was failing.

The blinking stopped. It started up again a full year later after several weeks of emptiness that culminated one flat and vacant weekend in the onset of something that seemed next-of-kin to narcolepsy. Everywhere we went, the car, the shops, the playground, anywhere . . . he went to sleep. Now he was six years old.

I lugged him round: a big, blond, baby weight, like a doll that had exceeded its powers. *The sun's too bright . . .* he said. It was so early in the year. The pale season. No one could accuse the sun of brightness. The sun had hardly woken up. This was not the neurotic flickering of the year before but the unconscious playing a tougher hand. I saw his eyes shutting and his head lolling like the dead, browned head of a sunflower towards the earth. Sleep is an active response to stress and the will to insensibility is often sensible. *Get out. Get out of here. Be gone.*

Eventually, the sleeping stopped. The blinking too. I breathed awhile, but not for long. Anxiety then moved into the nose in the shape of a loud, companionable sniff. The ears, the nose and throat make up a bond, a knot of closeness along which information is freely shared. Kids pick up fast. His friends were puzzled. *Why d'you make that funny noise?* they asked. Garland is good with words. He described it as a pancake up his nose. Choosing a pizza carefully from a menu, he said, *I don't like it when the cheese spreads out like a land mass.* In my imagination, the cheese, the pancake and the sniff were coalescing, all of the same white matter moving in readiness to smother us. I tried nasal sprays of salt, doses of antihistamine. I tried patience, and quickly, after that ran out, coercion. *Please stop.* I said, *Please stop.*

I can't. For a six-year-old, he had a point.

Then Garland started eating things. The sniffing stopped the day he swallowed a green plastic grape and thought that he would die. We looked out for the grape, but it had gone. It was not seen again. I reassured him that he would live but I could tell that he did not believe me. I was his mother. I would say that. We had never pretended his father wouldn't die though we did everything we could to stop it and he had heard that many times. It was part of the story we were making as we went along and it was as far away from fiction as we could get.

After the grape, he told me he had eaten a piece of Lego. It was red Lego, very small and he conceded it could have fallen among the other tiny pieces of bright red Lego on the bright red tray he was playing on and be lying there still. He agreed that it might be camouflaged and that he might not recognise it if he saw it again, but it was also possible that he had eaten it and therefore he would die.

Next, one lunchtime, he told me he had swallowed a chicken bone. As he spoke, his voice pitched without effort and his breathing was easy as a man on a stroll. I told him he had not swallowed a chicken bone. I told him the chicken they served at school contained no bones and was as far from a live bird as might be found, being flesh made paste and he would do far better to be vegetarian, but again he did not believe me as there remained the probability, the maybe likelihood, that he had swallowed it. He kept returning to the chicken bone as theme and I was rattled by the constant need for vigilance so tried to let it pass. I did not want to give it my attention. I wished the whole thing gone. It was then, the tummy aches started.

The tummy ache was real. As real as blinking, sniffing, and swallowing were real. *It's my normal tummy ache*, he would say, resigned, even though it had only just begun. Ten times a day or more, a gastric spasm right in the middle of the body at the point where you might run a string through the centre of a paper doll to spin it. In Ayurvedic medicine this will be the site of something. In voodoo, it is where the pin goes in. It is a generic point, the point a child will indicate if they wish to declare a problem of the self. *Here!* I held off going to the doctor, but the tummy aches got worse. In the night, he would wake me many times with what he called *a really bad tummy ache*. In the morning, there it was again, unwelcome. He was stoical, accepting of the situation. Old before his time. *It's just my tummy ache*.

He was anyway of the age for fears. Ordinary fears could make you weak enough. I knew how fear could come upon you, drop into the stomach like a flap of air to open up a space further to fall that was hollow, draughty, and unstable. I'd learned this through experience. The best friend at primary school who blanked me without warning on a Monday and kept it up for days – *maybe this was what a friendship was?* The girl who came to beat me up – *being quick was better than being clever*. The boy who'd stared at my chest in the tight sweater, the one I'd liked until I saw him looking – *how was a girl supposed to be?* There are so many things to fear . . .

Age five, children learn the world is not secure. Garland had good reason to know this. His path up to this point had been far from normal, yet the role of *normal* in any childhood must have its daily due. Age five it ratchets up. How to exist with others yet still find space to work out who you want to be. The whole, damn, socialising, other-people thing. It is as important as letters and numbers. School is just one place to learn. None of it comes easy.

Priya said my house was boring and she doesn't want to come any more.
Jamie will only do the thing he wants and never the thing I want.
I didn't understand what Miss Freeman said and she got cross with me.
Mikayla keeps saying all the paper aeroplanes I make are hers.

It is in separation that we see each other. That had been my first clear thought when he was born. How finally I could gauge what lay between us as a span or range to be explored, a landscape tested for viewpoints, outcrops, risks, and falls. Now I could speak of him and show him off with pride. Even when newly born and first unscrolled, arms wrapped around, we acknowledged the fact of our apartness. He was himself. *Garland*. Solo. Voyager. His ever being part of me had been transient, over as soon as he emerged. I was his caregiver/caretaker/not-forsaker, but Garland's whole being from the beginning pointed outwards and away from me to independence. It was a flowering-out kind of being. Mouth opening and closing, hands opening and closing, eyes opening and closing, his fingers curling like the blue-green tips of ferns in the *Encyclopaedia Botanica*. I saw the way his eyes, as soon as they could focus, looked round at everything, including us, with liberal pleasure. His prelapsarian instinct was not to cling but *move*. All we could do was root for him and cheer him on. I understood that he liked the world and what he most liked about the world was knowing that Sam and I were in there somewhere, even when not in sight. I was a node or plug of being to which he could return. His mother.

An island to be circled and kept in view. The infant phase, where he cried when I left the room, seemed short. It was as if he went through it for form's sake. Because that's what children do.

The outward impulse ceased. A switch turned off. To be out of sight was to be obliterated. *Stay!* became the norm. Or *Stay!!* Or even *Stay!!!* The interjections multiplied, ever more urgent. I did not leave his side. There was a time he would not let me leave the room. Then, I could leave the room but not the house. All absences became suspect. All transitions were scrutinised. To leave was wanton. To go was void. To go was to have never even been.

Taking the bins out meant taking the bins out forever in a purgatory from which there was no remission. There was no future and no past in this scenario, only a present ripe with impending absence. I do not remember how long any of this went on. A long time, a short time, it made no difference, it was all just time. And distance, well, distance is just distance.

The bins were right outside the door. Garland would watch me from the window. I eyed him back. The middle distance is the view I carry with me always. Between us stretched the universe in its entirety as known and nothing outside of it could be imagined. How small it was, and circumscribed and yet we could not even dream its edges. Like the oscillation between two poles, the air hummed like wind in a high wire. From not so very far away, five metres, six perhaps, I waved to him.

Funambule. Foo-nam-bool.

Now Garland is walking ahead of me on his way to school, making the plosive sound of the word with his mouth just for the fun, tasting the long vowels that formed between his lips like smoke rings. He seemed to float, slightly off the ground in a distempered haze. The air is warm, no vapour.

Funambule . . .?

I'm just excited. I don't know why.

Turns out *funambule* is French for tightrope walker. I didn't know this and for sure neither did he, he doesn't speak French, but I do, and it sounded familiar, so I looked it up. It was one of his words picked up from somewhere, like *miscreant* or *authoritarian*. His body bashes into mine as he walks. He was sticky and I was sticky and as we went along, we stuck.

I knew the feeling. Excitement. Unknown, unnameable, and anxious that came from some place you couldn't put your finger on but set off long and jangling spasms deep in the muscle. At his age, I'd felt it too. I'd shake my right arm in a compulsive tic that rippled wave-like, shoulder down to finger as if to shoo off some benighted spark. It was thrilling and at the same time, frightening, like a neurological bell, or an alarm – that sounded joy or fear – *which was it?* – hard to tell. At night and half asleep it came again. *When would it stop?* The body scarcely knows itself at times, not then and not much better now. *Why should it ever stop?* Connectors are firing all the time. Some miss their mark. It meant I was alive. *Growing pains*, my parents said in response to my suggestion that I might have Parkinson's. What did they know?

Garland's disease bank is more flamboyant now than mine was then. Of course it is. How could it be otherwise? Typhoid. Malaria. Fear must have its fix. *Funambule*. Everything he does is designed to activate the air around him. For Garland all information was readily transmutable as weapon. Garland raced through *A Dictionary of the Human Body*. After a small bout of something not so bad, he pulled diphtheria out of his bag and waved it like a silver trophy to get my reaction. Diseases were our test. The risk – or was it threat? – that he would be taken from me. *What are you gonna do then, eh?* – or *How will you protect me now?* Death was an intruder who moved by stealth. We could be jumped at any moment, we both knew that. Learned it some time ago.

Dark and slim: the bodies of anxiety made a nest of elvers, each with its own mottling. The chicken bone, the grapes, the sniff, the tummy ache, were so tight-knit they could not be picked apart. What was cause and what was root? What was head and what was tail? Where to begin? How to untangle them, drag them to light and lay them out in air?

Now we were two years in. One Monday, I took him to a doctor. She picked up fast, moving into language that was aimed at Garland and included him, yet circled his encampment lightly at a distance. I told her about Sam's death and how we still lived inside the space it made. I told her about the plastic grape, the Lego and the chicken bone. I took a sample with me. The grape was warm and sticky in the palm. We laughed as we passed it from hand to hand, huddled like archaeologists over a find. Garland laughed too.

Stupid grape, he said.

Stomach acid will have dissolved this long ago, but yes, it's something to think about.

She asked him to lie on the couch and poked his tummy. She told him about the thin, white threadworms that could come out of your bottom at night if you were lucky enough to have threadworms. *Very common*, she said. His eyes widened. She had his interest now. I almost wished there could be threadworms to distract us, but more to have some root, some wormal cause for all this business to which you could

114

prescribe a drug. Grief is high-grade instability. Alcohol is the drug of choice for this, but not for children. She described the Sellotape test to catch the little threadworm eggs. His eyes grew wider still and so did mine. We looked at each other across the room.

Suddenly he'd had enough. He did not want to be poked or held or spoken to. Enough. *You're fine*, the doctor said. He yawned and hugged me. *I think you're fine*. A sudden, collapsing tiredness came over him. I felt the weight of it as he leaned onto my neck.

Fine.

In the doorway as we left, I had a conversation with the doctor that Garland did not catch.

What were you talking about? he asked.

We were just checking that we understood each other.

And you had?

Yes, we had.

I am fine?

You are fine.

The tummy aches stopped. They did not return, but still we were not done. One morning, out of nowhere, he said, *Yesterday at carpet time I thought I was going to die.*

For the first time, he would not release my hand to enter class. He cried and had to be prised away just like the boy we'd watched with interest in the playground only the week before.

Why is that boy crying?

It will pass, I said to him. *It will all pass. You are working it out. It will all pass.*

Where does loss live? That was my initial question. Now we know.

13

At 6 a.m., I wake with the muffled head of the morning after. My vision is mid-tone. Not much is registering but I'm at home so I can handle it. I haven't had coffee, so am not in any way awake. I walk like a woman shackled, down to pee. I don't need to think. I know the way. It's my own house. I can pee blind and everything else blind. It's all there: the step, the stool, the door, familiar shapes made mysteriously soft and grainy, but the cones and rods are jumbled, and the muted light is pricking out red and green and black plasma instead of setting the room out clearly for me to see. When first awake, we are unmoored.

Now we are five summers in, or is it six? I can't keep track. Time passes but refuses to roll. It sticks, snagging at random on things that get in the way. These are the final days of June. The holidays are soon approaching. School will be out. And then we leave. We're going to spend the summer on an island.

*

Children think childhood is a long form game. Not so. By ten I'd lived in many different houses. Garland has lived in one. Our house was a stackable puzzle on three levels in which we had worked out our existence by experiment in close proximity. Our entanglement was formalised by our location. We shout to each other all the time from room to room, me from below and Garland above, or in the kitchen, elsewhere, anywhere.

Its architecture matched our pairing, initially by chance, then by routine. Two bedrooms, large and small. Between the sleeping rooms there was an open landing. A square window set into the floor allowed daylight to shine into the bath below and light to radiate up at night, illuminating the space between us. I put that window in some years ago, fusing the daily shower in my imagination with Danae and the rain of gold, but it never worked like that. The London light is flat. It doesn't stretch to allegory.

Two staircases, remnants of previous house conversions, set out against each other at a tangent. Two doors: one front, one back, matched by two corresponding sets of stairs, one to the road, the other to the garden, more of a fire escape, ending in a soft mulch of dirt and leaves.

The house had always felt vertiginous, as if a cliff had been repurposed as a building, in which we were always climbing, going up or down, not light, but clumsy, scrabbling for purchase, to answer the door, skidding to reach for the discarded bag, or shoes or keys or something else we had forgotten on the ground floor. Its steepness encouraged Garland to make a cable car for snails with an oatcake box as carriage that ran the whole descent along a single string. He lined the box with leaves but weighing up the risks – the snails would fall to their deaths upon the alpine stair – took the carriage down after a dry run, but the string remained a long while, getting in the way.

The house at this early hour is loose. Its edges misalign. Reaching for the cereal on top of the fridge. I think of the bowl that fell and cracked my head the year before, to launch a skinny rill of blood into my mouth. Blindly I fumble for the box and like a firework primed and ready, it bursts and splits in two as if there was a dual quality to everything, animate, innate and interlocking, dormant until a given moment. *Now*. Something shoots out, a live thing suddenly freed, and in the dark my heart jumps too, out of my mouth and into the world so fast it takes my breath. The animate part races across the table, down one leg and into the space behind the dishwasher. *It's just a mouse.* The box has birthed. Its job is done.

The day spills before I am ready. Mice are supposed to be fast, but this one travels in slow motion. My night-vision is lagging. I see it, but not really. I see a proxy. A mouse that has swallowed a mouse, like the drawing in *The Little Prince* of the snake that swallowed an elephant. I assign a picture of a mouse to the scene because my understanding has yet to catch up with my eyes. A mouse idea is substituting for a mouse.

My eye fixes her like a drone to its target. She moves across the kitchen in clear, straight lines, down and along, along, and down, close-hugging table and wall, her body a streak of warmish energy, guided at a point near the nose by the small capsule of her head that contains her brain, that fires the thinking, shitting, breathing, fucking, eating organs. It's a vulnerable little head. *Soft beast . . .* An owl pellet is the same shape as a mouse. An owl pellet is a joke on a mouse, being the rusticated remains of heads and wings and husks and claws, cleverly rearranged mouse-wise after a devouring.

I imagine crushing her head between finger and thumb. A hard nip and her skull would splinter against soft matter. I do not do this. I'm allowed to imagine. Maybe it would be harder. Maybe it would take more than a nip. Maybe I would have to work at her resistant body and she would fight to the death for her life. But first, I'd have to catch her. It was this mouse we heard last night behind the fridge, like Josefine the Singer in the Kafka story, trilling and chirping and showing off. Josefine the exception, knowing so well her music's power and knowing too that when she goes, the music would also disappear, who knows for how long, right out of the middle of our lives.

Garland, upstairs, missed everything. He said that from the kitchen, I made a high-pitched noise like a fire alarm. We had an argument about this later. We argue over all small things. His stories are never the same as mine. This one is mine. In my memory, it was different. In my memory, I was silent.

The kitchen smelt of mouse. The box went in the bin. Garland came downstairs and was unhappy at the lack of cereal. He was less invested than he might have been in the violent cosmic act of splitting and not inclined to compromise. Bad grace. No toast. Post early-morning fission, I too am brittle. I lose my temper, gain it, and lose it again. This is the wear and tear of us. The rub. It's often how it goes these days.

I know it's wrong to swear in front of children. I try to think of other words that would do as well but none of them come to my mouth at the right moment and the word sticks like a piece of potato that is too hot, too big. My mouth is full already. I try leaving the room, but there is nowhere to go. The other room is steps away. I cannot leave. After some minutes on the doorstep, I'd have to come back in. That is inconvenient. *Where to go in an argument with your sweary mouth in your own house.* It seems a particular conundrum for a single parent. *Self-control*, said a wise friend. *What about self-control? Ahh. Yes. That one.* I do not beat myself up at my lack of self-control. I do, though, fret about it through the day and later, when Garland comes home from school, he gets to hear my true and well-prepared apology delivered directly to his face. He looks puzzled. *Did you swear?* That clever trick. To hear and not quite listen. To listen and not quite hear.

It's time to go. Transitions are always difficult for us. As we separate into our different worlds, me off to work and him to school, we become, briefly, our worst selves. So many things to do at the same time, and all of them down to me. So now, in no apparent order: *Keys. Phone. Coat. Bag. Lights. Bike. Garland.*

On the radio, the newsreader is interviewing a Swiss ecologist. *Activists in Switzerland held their second 'mourning ceremony' on the evaporating Pizol glacier in the country's Glarus Alps on Monday. The glacier has lost up to eighty per cent of its volume since 2006.* It is the last item before the round-up, in the slot reserved for things that are not immediately classified as news. Her tone is one of mild concern. *As someone who sees the damage at first hand, how worried are you?* It's half past eight. Garland is still looking for his shoes. He looks distracted, but I know he's listening. Garland is always listening. He takes it in.

Garland's world at this point was stable but opaque. The mystery of others, however young, is worth preserving to a degree. My knowledge of Garland's world had remained the same throughout his first six years of primary school. He went to school with the others at nine and came home at end of day. On his return, he would be hungry, and a range of overlapping moods could be expected that impacted heavily on mine: happy, tired, sad, wild, confused, proud, elated, crushed, triumphant, maddened. Emotionally, he was profligate. Volatility was in his nature. The first hour was a roller coaster and after that, things settled, or if they didn't, you held on tight until they did. We were a dyad, stuck together. One plus one, but not in any sense a sum. Nobody said it would be easy.

What had he learned in these few years? One day, quite early on, he brought home a new mantra. *I am brave. I am special. I am unique. I am loved.* When questioned, he said airily . . . *Oh just some basic truths we did today.* For a while I took this mantra and went around with it fresh upon me like a new hand salve. It was good to have these propositions presented in the same voice as facts, like the present participle, or pyroclastic flow.

He learned about friendship and tried out different modes of kindness. He learned to recognise a bully and what language to use against them. He learned not to *be* a bully – a key lesson and not an easy one. He learned to write, to read, to add and multiply. He learned to join in well enough to pass at games, played football, rounders, cricket and Capture the Flag. He made parachutes from plastic bags and weights and threw them from windows with no discernible drag and that was called Physics. He learned History mainly from books at home and Geography, at first from maps and after that, from screens.

Garland was experiencing the world in ever greater increments. He was less interested than he used to be in cars and toys and things that were to hand. He was well beyond the point of *ball* being represented by the word *ball* and a drawing of a ball at rest on its own shadow, and near the point where a cluster of balls locked in a rigid, grid-like frame stood for a molecule of carbon in the form of graphite as found in pencil. That was Chemistry. The pencil at least was to hand.

Time for him extended on a fitful slide, from geochrono-metric scale, condensing to the ever-present moment, while size contracted from the oceanic to the atomic. Unreach-ability was in his sights, his targets linked only by orders of magnitude and distance from him in the imagination, including, these days in seeming random order, the Creta-ceous period, volcanology, the fall of Rome, far galaxies as seen by Hubble, but most compellingly of all for him, and most mysterious, the sea.

Garland carried in his head a chart of the deep, the one with all the zones. The Sunlight zone, the Twilight zone, the Midnight zone, the Abyssal zone and at a point so far removed it was hard to get your head around, the Hadal zone, the half-seen, half-imagined trenches of the ocean floor. Moving between the sea's depictions brought him foursquare against its mystery: the dirt-grey horizontal slab that was the Atlantic roaring on a wild day, rendered as diagram, in vertical bands of blue and green shading to sightless, lightless, never-fading black.

He watched the usual Ocean programmes on repeat like other children. *Octonauts*, *Blue Planet I* and *II* and *Finding Nemo*, in search of life forms stranger than he could make in his imagination. They kept on coming. Tube worms that lived on boiling vents at three miles down. Mudskippers dancing on meniscus. Remipedia. Blind! Venomous! Hermaphrodite! Those three words are enough for any creature. All praise for Remipedia! Garland was transfixed. Like a fisherman trawling the waters, he brought to light three-minute treasures found on YouTube. *Insane Shark Clips. Ten Best Squid Facts. More Epic Fails.*

He shows me the latest viral offering – he will not want to share his finds for long and later I may not wish to see the things he finds. A giant shipworm dragged from the depths is stripped from its shell on camera. The biologist works at the bivalve like a mechanic. First, he cracks its salicaceous shell with two sharp hits like taps on a hard-boiled egg. Next, he upends the creature, shakes it hard. The camera wobbles. Pauses. *Ohmygodalmighty.* Out slides a worm so slick and liquid-quick he almost drops it: more than a metre long and wet all over. Someone off camera swears. The camera steadies, pulls itself together. This is *Biology*. The bivalve is thick as the arm of the biologist. The creature is more compelling than a live thing has a right to be. *They eat wood*, says Garland, hunched to the screen in awe and whispering now. I nod. *Sweetheart*, I say, *the world is stranger than we can imagine . . . and this is just YouTube.*

That much had Garland learned. *What had I learned in all this time?*

So many things. I learned that distance is relative to your position in space. I learned that two is enough. I learned that on any line between two points, there's room for infinite expansion.. Hugged tight, Garland was three centimetres from my heart. That's not a metaphor, I mean a full embrace.

I did wonder sometimes in these years what he might be going to school *for*. He did not learn to draw or paint or how to raise his voice in song. He joined no choirs and school taught him little of music. He worked out war from his own games much like the others and, unlike the others, he had extensive knowledge of death before he started school.

This period of Garland's schooling was about to end. A couple more weeks and it would be over. The island, such

as we knew of it, was small. We'd looked it up but not much
else. A rock protrusion, set on the edge of the North Atlantic.
Volcanic, intrusive igneous with sedimentary traits, dimensions X by Y and population Z. That was the sum of what we
knew. A shore is a line on a map, an island is a point. It is a
full stop.

ISLAND

14

A fathom (noun) is 1.8 metres of water. To fathom (verb) is to understand a problem after much thought.

It was a woman who first mapped out the Atlantic. Marie Tharp was an oceanographer in the 1950s. Of all the waters Tharp plotted, the Atlantic remained her favourite. *It's such a nice symmetrical ocean*, she told the *New York Times* in 1991, *I felt sorry for the people who had to do the Pacific – it was so much more complicated*. Tharp was an explorer as much as she was a scientist. She mapped the sea floor out by hand. Without ever travelling to her destination, she got there first.

Tharp's early work was driven by data from small boats sailing back and forth across the ocean, taking echo soundings, and feeding the numbers back to her office in the Lamont–Doherty Earth Observatory at Columbia University where she laid them out like beads in rows to see what they could tell her. They told her a great deal. The numbers made a topographic record of the ocean floor in two dimensions.

Sound travels faster in water than in air. A sonar ping can register a point on the sea floor as a single unit of abyssal depth, and then another . . . and then a whole lot more. Reading the numbers off at each location, Tharp traced the seabed out in strands from one side to the other in sweeping avenues, plotting its inclines, peaks and drops. Out of this laborious process, she joined the dots to make a set of ocean profiles. Porto to Martha's Vineyard was one long sonar sliver. Dakar to the Lesser Antilles a fluid single span. Compiling all the profile data made a map. First a chain of mountains materialised, and then inside that range, a valley, followed by trenches, gullies, rifts and plains, plateaus. Here was a landscape never seen before.

Small boats. Big ocean. The early work was slow. Echo sounders were linked to a ship's electric power and any power fail could interrupt the signal to leave a gap. Where there were gaps, there was hypothesis. Nothing. One hypothesis could span many nautical miles.

The history of maps is full of blanks and what do we like to do with blankness? Fill it in. Artists turned centuries of ignorance to their advantage through ornament, embellishment and sheer invention. The sea throws up so many things to be imagined . . . how to resist? A great white whale, a plague ship, a sea-serpent, a long-imagined isle, a siren opening her mouth to sing. Sometimes Poseidon turning up himself. In the single channel between Scylla and Charybdis are whole libraries of competing monster stories.

The sea is the last unmapped unknown, the most impenetrable of all. Three-quarters of the ocean floor is still uncharted. For Tharp, imagining was not an option. The cartographers at Columbia couldn't make it up. Where there was nothing, there had to be something. On earth, there's always something. *Mare incognitum.* No data. Only sea.

There were few females doing the work back then. The Navy did not hold with women on boats – they brought bad luck to ships so weren't allowed. Pearl Harbor was the reason women got a foot in the door and Tharp didn't get to sea at all until 1968. She stayed on land, working for years with her colleague, Bruce Heezen, he on the research ship *Atlantis 1* and she in the office with her maps. Slowly, in solid, steady partnership, they traced the Mid-Atlantic Ridge, Tharp taking Heezen's soundings, plotting, drafting and redrafting as the technology improved and more accurate numbers came in. It was a young science, all to play for. The numbers just kept coming in.

Tharp had a systems brain in the new dawn of systems technology. She fingered the sea floor out in darkness, working the intervals between number and three-dimensional form to generate the seabed sight unseen through data, guesswork, guided hunch and vast reserves of knowledge. Soundings without the ability to interpret them are just numbers on a chart. Like early observers of far galaxies, Tharp knew where, and how to pay attention. The key lay often in the anomalies, noting down differences in scale, similarities in pattern and chasing down those thrice-checked, congruent, magic points where all the numbers met, and all the dots aligned like stars. An astronomer can look at a planet and make assumptions based on existing data and knowledge of other, similar planets. The astronomer has a telescope at least. Tharp had no such tools and no such data. The undersea was the underbelly of the earth. It was a tombstone environment, way out of sight.

The first Tharp–Heezen maps were contour ones, but

slowly they worked out how to transcribe the ocean profiles into pictures, enlisting the help of artists to flesh them out in three-dimensional form. This is what drawing does. It redescribes the world so we can see it differently. To understand how the land lies, sometimes you have to see it from a distance. Her maps were many metres long. In a photograph of Tharp from her time at Columbia, they span the room. She sits among them as they slide across the desk in giant sheets.

Early research was driven by military and corporate interests. Maps of the ocean floor in the 1950s were classified and not for public use. A physiographic map describes the terrain as if seen from the air. It brings the invisible to light. Here was a live source that could be published. The ocean floor could be imagined and once imagined, explored. Once explored, it could be seen.

The Tharp–Heezen project, *Physiographic Diagram of the North Atlantic Ocean* (1957), ink on paper, still holds much of its power. In parts, it's Middle Earth. You think to look for fires and forests, castles and goblin hordes across a vast plain pocked with volcanoes and gigantic valleys, scored down the middle by a chain of mountains unrecognisable as any mountain range on earth. Seen at close hand, it's fantasy. You could be anywhere. The surface of the moon and the sea floor seem much the same. Land frames the sea on either side like brackets. The blotchy clump that constitutes Newfoundland curls like a comma at the edge. The tip of Cornwall stubs its toe top right. The map is printed Admiralty colours, clean and plain. Water is designated blue, and land bleached yellow ochre, and where a seamount breaks the waves, the colour tips as one state shifts into another, wet to dry, to make, like a miracle, an island. Yellow dots, hard to pick out, scatter the mid-Atlantic waters. Islands are often fairly young. They are ephemeral. Formed by volcanoes pushing up against the weight of water pushing down, they bear the wounds of their adventures. The energy required to make any moves at all in these conditions is cataclysmic. Rocks lie where they fall, and as with any distant planet, the ground is deserving of intensive study. The Canaries are a set of active stalagmites. Small blocks of text are orphaned on the surface, all at sea.

And much like Middle Earth too, the deep was a contested world. Most geophysicists of the time were *fixists* who thought that land, being rock, the fundament on which we live, was structurally static. Tharp was a pioneer, a *drifter*. She knew that land was mobile, volatile. She was convinced of the existence of the Mid-Atlantic Ridge but had to work to persuade Heezen. *Girl talk*, he called it first of all. *Girl talk*. But the numbers kept on coming. They pointed to a gap, a rift, a great valley in the middle of the sea. Back then you could be fired for being a *drifter* and the resulting academic feud got Tharp, not Heezen, sacked. She was the softer target. Withdrawal of support forced them to take the work elsewhere, outside the institution. Tharp took it home with her. The North Atlantic was mapped from a living room in South Nyack.

Many things followed the publication of the map: Bell laboratory cables, the developing science of tectonophysics, marine exploration, tsunami early warning systems . . . Tectonic plates are thought to move at a rate of four centimetres a year. Since 1957, when *Physiographic Diagram of the North Atlantic Ocean* was first published, that's over two and a half metres at the bottom of the sea and widening.

Tharp does not figure in any of Garland's encyclopaedias. Alexander Graham Bell is there and Jacques Cousteau, the film-maker and oceanographer who set out first to prove her wrong, then realised she was right. Tharp remained a footnote, her name and reputation growing – slowly – at pace with continental creep – until in 1997 she was named one of the four greatest twentieth-century cartographers by the Library of Congress.

They say that more people have visited the moon than the bottom of the sea – one of those sweeping statements that seems to point to deeper truth, but hard to work out exactly what. For the Challenger Deep, at nearly seven miles down, it's twenty-two and rising year on year, though no one of course has walked there. Twenty-four have travelled to the moon so far, but only twelve have stood on it and from there, turned to look back at us.

Tharp, the cartographer of the Atlantic Ocean, outlived her colleague Heezen by many years and kept on working. Nine years after her death, she got her recognition. This time, it was a true and proper accolade, an honour very far away, befittingly out of reach. Tharp is a crater on the moon.

15

Everyone has their own horizons, the favoured points at which the eye takes rest along a line that feels most like or unlike home, depending on where you're running from or escaping to. The curving strip of sand at Provincetown. The icy waters of Deep Bay. The Kyle of Tongue in winter. The deceptive line made by the Channel at Kent, its tameness an illusion. Dutch technoscapes, flat and hydrologically compressed, dragged from the sea by force. These are some of mine. You will have yours.

A horizon seen from the shore is an emotive line. To see it is to go on a journey, cover the distance in one breath out and then along without space for thought to intervene. It is a journey to which we are so accustomed that we do it in our dreams. *As far as the eye can see* we say, by which we think we mean a long way but really, it's not so far. The horizon sets our limit relative to the uncertain spot we hold, a cliff, a pier, a ferry . . . the closest thing within the upturned bowl that constitutes our understanding and maps onto a flattened curve that, by extension, bounces off in time and space elsewhere in our imagination, first to low-lying clouds, to stratus, stratocumulus, ice storms at altitude, then on to cirrus, up to the narrow curve of air, mere fingernail, the edge of space.

The sea is the place to watch the world in motion. A ringside seat. Warm air rising, water falling, clouds being hauled across as if on pulleys, all light and heat and energy compounding exponentially to multiply by factors of itself. The sea regenerates the earth. In framing it we set great store by its proportions, sky to sea. I take a photo. Shift the camera up a bit, along, then down to get it right. Above. Below. Not satisfied, I take another, then a few more. I'm still not happy. We draw the horizon as a clear line across a picture and sink the sun in spectacular fashion down behind it. But the sun does not sink anywhere on earth, and sky and sea are twins, two systems that move in circulation, setting the hydrosphere to work, celestial, terrestrial, out and along, along and down, and round of course, as ever on an island – round and round.

This is the final stretch. We're on a boat. The journey felt like days. The ferry only takes an hour. On the crossing, Garland, the figurehead, holds to the white rail. He could be any child, a local boy, squinting against the sun under his cap. He is impatient, wanting to see the island first, and when he does – a faint brown smear that holds like a slug to the line of the horizon – he's not impressed. No matter. We have *six weeks*! This is a luxury. The time before us gleams like the flat sea. The air is fully charged with fuel. The ferry steams its way through blue.

It's easy to imagine you're the first: first to set eyes on things, a sudden peak, a flash, a waterfall, a view glimpsed from a passing car. When something catches your eye, it's yours – or good as yours. Some people really *are* the first and stake their claim as conquest, but they are few. The rest just follow on. All views have been taken in before by others, mostly unknown and unrecorded. *Think of an island.* We are all first-comers in our own imagining. First sightings are our prize. No one will see the island Garland sees.

We left the mainland with no undue ceremony. There was no ticket booth, no snack bar, just a line of cars. A message board that flashed in caps, marked our departure. *FAREWELL* it said. *NO IDLING*. We were the only passengers on foot. That was the first thing we noticed. Marsha, our host, is there to meet us off the ferry. She is a smiling woman with a dark fringe sliced reassuringly in a dead straight line as if with a knife, and next to her, her daughter Ellen stands like her slighter shadow, same fringe, same smile, more reticent, with skinny plaits that bounce around her shoulders as she walks. Giant dragonflies, big as Garland's hand, spring fresh from the warm tarmac all around us, skimming the pools of iridescent oil and alighting on the bumpers of the red and blue trucks that stand in line, waiting in turn to board and radiating warm-engine energy straight back to the sun. Trucks and insects are bullish here. That was the second thing we saw. They come in two sizes, large and extra large. Garland is mighty pleased. We have arrived. We all shake hands. Whole streams of talk pour out of us in our excitement at being on land.

Garland had slept the previous night in the departure lounge. I had not slept. On the plane, two heads as one, but bodies wildly out of sync, we'd peered from the narrow, recessed window. It was a restricted view, the far corner of a provincial airfield. Not so much to see. A windsock held to the line of horizontal. A paper cup rolled by. We watched the wheels grind up the landing strip to raise a fine-grain residue of dust, made up of sand, small feathers, seed heads from grasses in the safety zone, skin from the hands of men at work, crushed glass, spilt oil and coffee. Beyond the point of no return, ascent kicked in under the ribs and held us up. We rose as weight, improbable as ever, and took the dust along with us as cargo.

Arrival was the opposite of landing. Arrival felt vertiginous, like cresting a mountain at a high point to find a sudden, unexpected view or further yet still to go. Six weeks on an island was a foreign body. It made a shape where time and place were cut exactly congruent and fitted neatly one inside the other. Back home, we'd blocked the trip in outline on the calendar, and watched in anticipation as if it might reveal something about itself ahead of time but it did not. The empty space inserted into the busy scribble pattern of our days made an austere shape that cracked the year like a rolling ice floe, long and white: long enough to divide it into the time preceding, and the time that followed – *before* and *after* – and easy, though very like inaccurate, to read as portent. *Under the right conditions, water freezing inside the smallest fissure can split a rock*. For me it was a working trip. I would be there to finish a convoluted project started then stopped, abandoned halfway through the previous year. I was not confident of its completion. Garland was coming with me. What he would do there, was unclear. For Garland it was simply summer. He was on holiday. Garland was ten. He could take care of himself.

Before we left, we'd followed the island roads on Street View. The rest was therefore in our imagination, blank. There were two roads, the 333 and 334. Street View is faithful to the road ahead, pares back the land to left and right and holds to a primary goal of destination. It failed to record the circling sea, the blazing bowl of sky, the skimming birds or sudden jets of sun. *Linear* is not the word to reach for on an island. Garland spun wildly in his seat.

The road turned right and split, one section forking down towards a jetty, the other curving to the hill. Neither route was marked. Both were dead ends. This was Whale Point Bay. All houses in the community converged around this axis.

I take a picture, Garland as usual, in the way. *What is there here to see?* It's getting late, the day has lost its heat. Coolness pulls up the whites and damps down yellows, leaching the latent warmth out of bare rock and lighting the landscape like a diorama constructed to show exactly how things are in a particular place, or used to be, or in this case perhaps more fittingly to show how certain salient features stayed the same and would not change.

What is an Island?
A portion of land entirely surrounded by water.

Seen from a single viewpoint, the facts on the ground are plain. A sheltering hill, a bay, some jetties, boats, a church. Houses in loose informal figuration. From this elevation, slightly raised, these are the main components, with all the anecdotal touches here and there: a tyre, a buoy, an upturned boat, abandoned coil of rope, set perfectly to scale. The houses are one-storey or two and built from template, made of wood as variations on each other in white or brown, each with a contrasting, painted trim in green or red as if to demarcate themselves in outline from the others and signal their identity in rudimentary form against the background rock.

The buildings are geometric, cast like blocks thrown down within a landscape that is otherwise devoid of lines, save for the sure one the sea makes, and yet the houses sit so sparsely over the ground, with so much openness between them that it is an easy thing in the mind's eye to rub them out, leaving a headland more or less unchanged since it was formed, apart from the tarmacked road that looks still new and trucks parked at uncertain angles here and there along the way.

What is an Ocean?
The largest division of the water.

These are the rudiments by which a place defines itself and thrives or grows, develops, slows, shrinks to a stub, or over time, is reinvented. Each element, each wooden house, each jetty, seemed in itself quite frail, and while clearly dependent on the others, made stronger by some margin, but even then, exposed – open in all weathers to the sea, to feast or famine, the ice that forms each year, the ferry that might not for some reason run that day, to vagaries of power supply, to fish, or lack of fish. Seen through a camera at the edge of rock, it's the precarity that sticks.

A church sits parallel, rectangular in frame. A plain white box with windows punched clean all along its length, its spire is a truncated stub that points in a pioneering way to heaven, but equally in sure-footed mode, and in the way it hugs the ground, attends to earth. The sun picks out the timber in the foreground, the pile of longer, leaning lengths and shorter stumps in heaps. And there in the middle – a red truck. This is the truck that will be ours to drive for the duration. It's the only red in the picture. It draws on the ambient, late accumulating light and soaks it up. Garland already loves the truck.

The scene is incomplete. The deep blue bay – *It's deep enough for whales of course*, says Marsha, laughing – is not in frame. There are no people in the picture.

A house sits on its own, apart. White with a green trim – this one is ours. It's like a ship, the way the deck goes part way round and rocks pile up beneath as if to hold it steady. A stairway rises to the front and another from the kitchen out to the side, with the whole frame raised on a wooden platform to accommodate the wildly uneven ground. Rocks and plants push up the most unlikely shapes, as if the landscape in these parts struggles to contain the two phenomena, vegetable and mineral, side by side and actively in competition. The hill is made of these twin forms heaped up in mounds and soft cascades, one on another, but quickly as it rises, the bushes – blueberries, we learn, primed and near-ripe for picking – fall behind, to leave a slope that seems from a distance, barren and void of life. A path cuts sharpened zigzags into rock and disappears. The sun is low. The sky at this hour is white.

If you could remove one colour from the world, what colour would it be?

Doing a workshop in Garland's school when he was younger, I brought in paper in many different colours, pastels and chalks and neon pens to supplement the usual HB pencil diet. There was a long pause. Twenty-eight heads. Silence in the classroom. They blinked but didn't move. They recognised this as the kind of question teachers lobbed in like a soft grenade occasionally to ruffle them and get their attention. It worked, annoyingly. What colour would it be?

Alma's hand went up. A hesitation. *Orange.* In the volley of discussion that followed, they fought over the question. They decided it could no way be blue or green. If the class had been asked to fight, they would have rallied round blue and green. Blue for water. Green for land. They were less clear on red, and yellow produced gridlock. It was harder than deciding what animal to do without if you had to do without an animal. That was a game they sometimes did in the playground.

I stand with Garland looking out. We gauge the span of water side by side, but it is black and reflects nothing. The sea has caught us, pulled us in again. From the deck, we look to a low island in the bay. There are no buildings on it, just a cemetery no longer now in use, old graves part-blended with the grass. Only in clear weather were they readable as individual and separate markers.

In that first hour we learn that like a ship too, a house on rock is mobile. It can move, change hands, be sold, packed up onto a truck, transplanted elsewhere, or in these parts, as Marsha tells us, be launched from another shoreline and sent on rafts across the bay. A home in one place might look wistfully to its former setting the following year. Light in those first few weeks would fall at an uncommon slant within until it settled. On a small island, where trees were scarce, with not so many people, all resources are held in common. Everything built could be rebuilt elsewhere and handed on.

Though nowhere near the shore at Small Paynes Landing – more than six years had passed and many thousand miles – I am transported back. We had arrived at a configuration that seemed, though unforeseen, immediately familiar. A wooden house, same sea, but different shoreline. This time we're on an island. This time the house is built on rock. This time there's something else, so slight at first, it takes a while to notice, put my finger on it. Could be a realignment of the view. A shift in frame. This time I'm in the scene. Not at the edge, the centre.

I look around for Garland to see what he has noticed, but what is there here for him to see? A basic house with two rooms up and two below. Time is an unfixed interval, a floating span. We are the constants here. Love is narrative. We write it as we go along. It was a mystery how any time at all had passed.

The stairs were the colour of wet brown dog. Now he has raced up them already. He seems at home. The new incorporates the old within itself and carries on.

On the fourth day, the neighbour comes to greet us, tells us the house had previously been in his family for generations. He points to a site a little further down and says it used to be *there* and before that, waving his hand towards the island of the abandoned gravestones, *there*. We ask where he lives now. He laughs and points in the direction of his current house, a bolder and more expansive version of the traditional footprint, white, with a double garage, boat, and smart new trim. *There!*

He brings us a gift of frozen, milk-white fish, so pale it's almost blue, sealed in a ziplock bag. Later, we put it in the pan and as it starts to warm, the fish, the fat, the heat and light set off a chain reaction in the kitchen that seems unstoppable. The air goes live with effervescent oil. It is narcotic. The house fills suddenly with sun, chased down by molecules of sea.

16

It's hot. When we wake, our bodies are already airlocked. 6 a.m. and the heat snaps on like a second skin, slightly tighter than our own. Within the hour, atmospheric pressure deflates us gently on the inside, but the bright light keeps us on high alert, eyes fixed to the horizon. Each day we wake, it is the same.

What are we doing? *Thinking?* A thought in sight of the horizon will not be the same thought at a computer. *Scanning?* What are we scanning for? Our eyes adjust poorly to an ocean surface. It resists us. We are drawn to its monotony yet fear its pull in the same moment. We're primed to respond so readily to differences in pattern, changes in colour, distinctive features in a landscape – that we will clutch at anything that passes for disruption within the sameness, a buoy, a bird, a line of weed that turns the water bronze, a sandbank spiking the pattern of the waves. *Nothing?* It's never nothing. The sea's blankness is a cover. The sea is not blank. Nor is it uneventful.

The sea is events all the way down. At its edge, I drink, am drunk and get drunk up. I never tire of looking at the horizon. I thought I would but have not yet. It is hypnotic. I vanish clean away. Viewed from the deck at Whale Point Bay I shake my eyes loose like drops over the water, followed by the spilled contents of my head. Garland chucks stones into the water. He's looking too.

The clothes on our backs are warm the moment we enter the sun. Stones and small ceramics hold their heat for hours. We expect lizards but see none. This is not the Mediterranean. It is the Atlantic Ocean. Latitude 49.6713° N, 54.2910° W. Underfoot is rock. It's warm as blood.

Garland knows mainly the totality of the present as it wraps round him. Right now that means the sun. He is fixating on the climate. He is a boy of many overlapping phases that come in low, like waves of varying intensities, each one different from the last but on the same trajectory. This is a new phase into which his other phases are subsumed and barely register. The daily sun is to him become a worry. On an island that's mainly rock, with so few trees, this is a problem.

He is attuned: always on high alert and picks up news from elsewhere all the time. So far this summer, it's been bad. *When will the news be different?* Garland wants answers. I have none to give. He cannot stop himself and like an itch he needs to reach, searches for record highs in other places. A summer of wildfires had torn down the Pacific coastal strip. Sea temperatures off southern California rose in May to an unprecedented peak, and in Los Angeles, the power kept going down, fuelled by a million air-conditioners surging in sync. In mid-July, the Arctic Circle tipped on the dataset to red to match the temperature of Spain. Greece simply burned and people ran away. China that summer was a great pot about to boil, a curving bowl that stretched from Kyrgyzstan to Khabarovsk. At home, it was the same, with just the place names more familiar. A blaze took seven square miles of moorland outside Manchester. *Ash fell like rain*, they said. Grassland at Wanstead Flats went up in flames and trees in Epping Forest turned to kindling, fanning the East End with oven heat, and threatening the industrial estates and houses on the suburban fringe.

I switch off the news, resolving to draw his attention in, and keep it for the duration fixed and fully local. An island is a limit unto itself. Unless you move in, take up residence and hang up your own flag, there is nowhere to go except back. On the ferry, all tickets were returns.

Garland was restless. In those first days he made unsettled weather. He moved cautiously in search of shade as if the sun could do him actual harm. His mood would rise and fall in opposition to the day's brightness. Pinning your happiness upon a blue sky is a fool's game but anxiety and impotence are a heady mix, and I was worried. I picked my way with care round conversations about the conflagration at the end of time but fast ran out of things to say to give him solace. *What will we say to give each other solace when the time comes?* Solace is needed now. We need new words, new forms of language for the young and people still to come. Like a child abandoned in an old people's home, Garland would weather-watch. *It looks like rain*, he said hopefully on coming to the window in the morning, or, more often, mournfully, *Doesn't look like rain.* While I took each bright blue sky as invitation and acceptance at the opening of a single curtain, he liked to see the clouds slide like a roof over his head. Rain brought him instant reassurance. *All will be well!* I worked hard in those early, sun-filled days to cheer him.

17

I miss you most at equinox
When, all things being equal,
Night has my left hand and day my right.
You always were more prone to seasons.

It is 21 June. The summit. The day the year falls away on both sides. I don't hold with anniversaries, apart from Garland's birthday, to which we all give praise and honour. A death day comes round once a year in passing, as does a wedding day, which I forget or then again remember, but can't think how to mark. Today, to get our bearings, we're going to walk.

We had come to the highest point on the island. Chunks of rock and scree sloped down in diagonal final reckoning and green-black firs clung vertical to the steep slopes on the north side. An island is a mountain with its foothills in another register beneath the sea. A mountain on an island is twice mountainous. From here the visible looks improbable enough. The invisible is scarcely to be imagined.

Look! I shout to Garland at the summit. *It is the same and different all the way round.*

Ascent was by a strip of track of some two hours. All views were at first obscure. Our new, stiff coats, not quite yet broken in, were pawed and snagged by branches and our ankles sliced by low birch twigs. As novice climbers we were zealous. We started out first thing and walked ourselves awake along the trail. The sun climbed with us and our mood rose directly in anticipation. We were already much too warm within the hour.

A gap of sky, seen first as a small blue patch, signalled the proximity of the summit when suddenly, with no apparent notice, a sharp incline, a sudden scramble up a gravel slope, the bushes fell away to leave the summit bare. The blue of the sky is an illusion. We all know that. Blue is just the colour given to distance. Not concrete in nature, it is abstract. In painting, blue is yonder, the colour that designates *elsewhere*. The sea and the horizon, both are awarded the special prize of blue.

We're not the first. Dragonflies are here again to meet us. The summit belongs to them if we are there to witness it or not. Gaudy and skittish, like false eyelashes at a party chasing glue, dragonflies have always been here, long before birds, and before the ancestors of birds, they surfed the playful zips and updraughts of warm air and metered out the tilt of day to night as the sun cued up the moon in readiness. In *Minecraft*, Garland says the dragonflies come big as birds. They spawn in prehistoric sizes, with giant wings in iridescent shades. Test pilots and pioneers, they hovered in display formation and dragged our attention rudely back from the horizon to hang six inches from our faces as if to say *Look here – not there!* They jump at the synthetic sounds our jackets make. We are, above all living things, *loud*. Before descent, we check each Velcro flap and pocket carefully, in case the energetic ones had stowed away. Garland is special nectar to them, his unformed prepubescent heat. They pause to fine-tune themselves mid-air in front of him.

What is the weather like in *Minecraft*? Lightning may be summoned manually. Fish are agitated after rain. Leaf fall is restricted. Land is readily hydrated. Garland's interest in landscape runs in parallel to his other interests. He loves to camp. Building a world comes readily to him and once dug in, he gladly puts in extra hours, constructing shelters, haunting familiar trees and burying whole regiments of enemies alive. *Minecraft* is a place as much as it is a game and Garland likes to spend time there, drawn to its vertical, windless rain and biomes of luminescent caves. How else might an urban child beat off a wolf, construct a ziggurat at home or raise high the roof beam on their own farm?

What is the sea like in *Minecraft*? Whales carve out replicas in water. Sea levels are maintained. Underwater visibility can be adjusted. Tridents may be re-enchanted. He followed its updates as they dropped like key additions to a creation canon. That spring alone had brought a fresh marine bonanza, of coral fans, kelp forests many metres long and waves of zombies, drowned yet relentlessly alive. Terrain appears in the game ahead as fast as a 'toon in a cartoon universe can lay down track in advance of a speeding train. The world comes into being block by block. Technically it was infinite, though in the early days, when sandbox worlds were way more primitive, *Minecraft* was only infinite in theory. As computers got faster, coordinates got larger and the *Minecraft* world became correspondingly less secure, leaving a hazy terrain far from a central spawn point in a flat world that was doomed to lagging, neatly underscoring the solipsism of a player at the centre of a domain subject to dissolution so far from its point of origin. Back then, this region was called, straightforwardly, the Far Lands. In later versions of the game, the code was tightened, to make the edges of the Far Lands more consistent with the near. Now you can fly there. A person could walk within the game for months. Someone is doing it now.

What is the sky like in *Minecraft*? Fancy skies can be downloaded. Clouds may be set to *off*. Fog is rendered horizontal. The sky, as we know, has limits. Seen from the summit, a panorama throws up our limitations plainly. We are front and facing creatures and feel the fixed terms of our condition. To see the world fully, we turn and turn again, as if only in turning, are reassured to find it all still there.

Garland is looking out to sea. The nape of his neck is landfall for my hand. The back of the head is blind. There, we are exposed.

I took a photo of Garland once when he was facing the wrong way. It wasn't a mistake, but the picture I meant to take. I liked it because the photograph contained his view. It stuck Garland and what Garland was looking at together like two dried flowers in a book. *Who dries flowers anymore?* This was his true and accurate rendition. No portrait. No messing about. No trying to read his face for clues. Mostly, everywhere I go, Garland is in the way. He is my companion obstacle. My view has him inside. He's either there in shot, or somewhere just outside the frame. It's hard to imagine the scenery without him. It's hard to imagine anything without him. That time will come. The photo points away from me. He's growing up. He looks elsewhere.

When he was eight, we'd spent a week apart. This was a new thing for us. A test. He passed, but I was lost without him in my field of vision, I decided to send him a photo every day; not general views of hills, in which he would have no interest, but specifics. Views of hills are for adults, who appreciate them. To enjoy a mountain is learned, whereas to enjoy the sight of a slug, it seems, is not.

- A fox-head marker carved into a wall.
- Dragonflies over a pond.
- The slug: a coin set by for scale.
- Dock leaves mined to skeletons by beetles.

Later, I found he did not look at them. His world was much more interesting than mine. I kept forgetting.

The back of the head is strange terrain. Well known but unfamiliar. Many things become apparent there without intention. Once on a station platform I watched the back of a lover's head as he walked away. I had time to notice the way his hair, a plain brown, pressed flat from sleep, coiled round his head like frost-formed fractals on a window. Nothing was said, but we both knew it was over. He was leaving. *Cue*. Turn and walk away. I was staying. *Cut*. It felt like the longest shot, but the train came on time and there he was, gone in a minute and the film over. In hospital, bored after an operation and waiting to be discharged, I studied the head of the nurse assigned to me, as a walker studies a map, saw how she pinned her hair up sight unseen to make a formless shape like a mat scratched loose by a cat, a shape that marked how spent she was, how tired each day. Some people remember important things. I say these are important things.

There is a list of images of the backs of heads. It's not so long and once you notice them, you're hooked. You look for more. Ray Lee Jackson's photo of Gertrude Stein is one. Hard to marry what is known of the weight and structure of a head – eleven pounds, two bags of flour – with this near-perfect sphere. Stein is a stone ball. A projectile waiting for a cannon. You can't imagine what such a head is thinking. Her hair is cropped in close and her ears tucked neat like a vole. It's a studio shot. She sucks all the air out of the picture without even trying. We're lucky not to see her face.

It's a niche list. There's not so many. That famous one – a painting, by Gerhard Richter of his daughter Betty, distracted and turning away from him. People like this postcard because that's what children do. Their attention shifts. They turn away from us. Then there is Caspar David Friedrich: he is the master of the form. There is a tiny painting by Friedrich, *Two Men by the Sea at Moonrise*. It's a mysterious scene. It shows a moonlit shore with two small figures centre stage, their backs to us. That's it. The picture cues up some connection. The men are dressed the same, stand close but not together. They could be friends, or brothers, but equally, they might be strangers, stopped on the road as travellers and struck for a moment by the view. We cannot know. The two men snag the scene and soak up all the dying light. Our thoughts get tangled up in theirs. We're stuck. We stand with them and stare at the horizon. In Friedrich's paintings, everyone looks the wrong way, or perhaps it's the right way, who's to say, but anyway, away from us.

In the photo, Garland is looking at a sculpture by Peter Fischli and David Weiss, called *Rock on Top of Another Rock*. This was a work that just appeared, in the way that public artworks can appear and then, after some months or years have passed, they go, and later still, you note their absence unexpectedly while cycling by and miss them afresh. Objects will often hold the memory of your first encounter, remind you of who you were back then and play it back. There's nothing else in the photo. No sky. No view. No setting to locate you. There's only rock. *Rock on Top of Another Rock* by Fischli and Weiss is a sculpture made of rocks. They're not fake rocks – they're real enough, transported in from Wales on massive trucks – but it's an artificial stack. One boulder has been balanced carefully upon another to make a megalith, a miracle of engineering that sets a granite stranding in the heart of London, held up by force of gravity as if by magic. Garland had been running round it laughing with his friend when suddenly winded, stalling for time, he stopped. Mid-flight, mid-chase, mid-circumnavigation. That's when I took the picture.

The horizon is a gift. A banded edge that orbits and divides the world into above and below. Islands, towers, tall buildings, or their equivalents allow the tracing of the world full circle. This is rare. Garland spins round to take it in and once he starts he doesn't want to stop. I share the feeling. At elevation, the brain struggles to translate the eye – or is it the eye that fails? Sight collapses over the distance back. The focus slips. There is no grip. It's all the same. An oscillation in the optic nerve sends ripples across available light. Windless and luminous, the air is hazy, like gauze pulled through the finest cosmic ring. The trail we had taken only an hour before was barely visible and all small paths had vanished, as if in a folk tale we had erased the memory of our journey even while walking and couldn't return that way again. The clump of houses that marked our start point, registered in the distance as dice thrown down, and the sky met itself neatly in a ring. No compass points, no items of particular distinction, only a rotating view though twenty miles of uninterrupted air.

These are the facts. We live on a sphere. A sphere has bounce. A sphere has spring. A sphere has limits and at the horizon the eye falls off the edge. So far so medieval. Flat Earthers, convening with your merchandise in some terrestrial car park – stop reading here.

18

Garland is in explorer mode. Idly one afternoon he goes on a hunt on Google Earth for other islands, the smaller and more remote for him the better, as if he has outgrown this one immediately upon arrival although he has in no way got its measure. This is the second week. Scrolling his way across the Atlantic, the screen is mainly blue. An island is easily missed. Ascension, Inaccessible, Santa Luzia, St Peter and St Paul, St Helena . . . all the saints, blessings upon them, their peaks converging skyward . . . on to St Kilda, not any saint at all, the remnant of an old volcano, long deceased, that spikes the North Atlantic a hundred miles from mainland Scotland as the crow flies.

Still anchored to the laptop and without moving from his position at the table, Garland goes further on his travels. He's found a website called Perpetual Ocean. Once discovered, he returns to it now and then, like a security guard will check the doors of a building at night, or a lighthouse keeper do the rounds in olden days. Perpetual Ocean is an animation made by NASA, that mashes real-time, ocean current data with computer models. For such a colossal pinball game, the sum of so much energy, it's strangely cool, and pictured on screen, serene to the point of soporific. A twenty-minute version runs on the NASA site, while a more dramatic trailer with variations in speed and revolution plays on YouTube. The globe is set to music, an ambient wash that's clearly a placeholder for sound which is to our ears unfathomable. We are accustomed to music with our nature media as a bundle of emotive content, a practice so hard-wired it's hard to undo or even to unhear. Music underscores the imagery of the natural world as narrative. There is no narrative to Perpetual Ocean save for the one encapsulated in its title: the sea as boundless, never-ending force. *What is the soundtrack for the turning world?* The crack of a rock face on the brink? A note played on a theremin matched to the pitch of calving ice? The hit of waves against a harbour wall? *Think of a melody . . .*

Perpetual Ocean sets the world to spool against its own negative. The sea is the star and here gets all the detail. The Gulf Stream is a complex twist that fuels the North Atlantic, then spins outward, oceanward from North Carolina, dragging more water with it than all the world's rivers put together. Sturdy, fast-paced, headstrong, we pray it never wavers. The Kuroshio, the Black Current, steams past Japan and heads north-east, to bring salt water warmth into the Pacific. Windy gyres ping from one land mass to another. Wave systems run east-west-east, along the equatorial line, cutting like dancers in and out of each other's moves. Currents bounce off Canada and minor vortices swing from the coast and out to sea. The inky blues are passionate. The whites, unstoppable. The closest match for all this visual energy, though from another register entirely, are Van Gogh's nocturnal skies of France, where clouds are painted as celestial wagon wheels in motion and spontaneous-combusting stars are hurled round a blazoned moon.

Land is given the colour and texture of damp sand, perfect for spades and sandcastles but otherwise left unrendered. Mountains are only lightly modelled, with few specific features. There are no conurbations, jungles, deserts, rivers, or any green at all. Land in Perpetual Ocean is empty and given a wet sheen like caramel or toffee.

In the kitchen we turn the ocean bubble music off. The globe becomes a silent ornament: a bauble on rotation in a black-tiled ballroom. Caught in a triple far remove – the house – the rock – the earth as seen from outer space – the horizon becomes a sweet and lovely circle that clicks on itself to close. It makes a kind of centre, ours, the one we know. This is our planet. To pick Perpetual Ocean up and roll it between your hands would be a pleasure. It would be glossy, frictionless – and lonely. You would be entirely alone.

The house stands open, doors and windows wide and air moves freely through its frame. The washing machine shifts onto spin. Wind flattens the hair against our heads, grass lies horizontal, and the front door bangs hard against the latch. We are assailed by currents at every level. The air expands the room. It's clean. I take a long breath in and another out.

Garland is bored now. He's made some local friends and heads outside to play. Meanwhile on YouTube, in the sidebar, seascapes mount. The titles are salve enough themselves. *Waves calm the heart . . . Ocean Sounds for Deep Healing . . . Twelve hours of Underwater Wonder . . .* I do not need to click on them to know their power. In Garland's absence, the algorithm takes me further out, to full immersion.

We lived outdoors. Garland in shorts and sandals. In March they said, the pack ice came. In April, icebergs arrived. By June they'd gone and by September – coming soon – we'd be gone too. Imagination stalled at winter. We were summer people, filed with the others passing through, destined to leave with far too many photographs to look at and thoughts not fully formed as pictures. Our days are blocked in solid light. Winter was separate from summer as night is from day.

Night comes in fast, and unimpeded. It gathers quickest in the hollows, settles like carbon, blooms in the cracks like moss and lingers least on surfaces freely available to the moon. All objects lose coherence. A rock is a rock till suddenly it's not, could be an upturned boat, a bush, a bear, and in the evenings, when we take leave of friends, they are already blurring even as we wave goodbye. At dusk, the wash of light that coloured rock so vividly as coral, is gone the moment you turn your head away. The ground falls back to shadow and suddenly as if on cue, all pinks are taken into sky and only the sea retains the memory of pink, reflected back.

Garland loves to drive the island roads at night. At night a passing car is an event. Headlights finger the road ahead in beams along the horizontal as if to flatten it. By day a cross-roads is a simple choice of right or left. It makes no difference, the roads come round eventually to meet again. By starlight, it is a staging post for ghosts, a tryst. We cut the engine out and sit and wait.

5 Rough Sea, Walton-on-The-Naze

19

Back home I have a collection of postcards picked up from junk shops along the way. The rule is they must cost almost nothing. They must be labelled *general view*. They give little away.

> A general view of Pontygwaith, 1920
> General view of Manchester Cathedral
> General view of Leith, from Leith Walk

A general view is a photograph without incident. Usually taken from a semi-high point, but not an aerial view. It is a topographic image, designed to give an indication of how the land lies. A rough guide only, no specifics. In a general view, there will be some basic parameters that might locate you. The ground is rock, the sea is calm, the village small, the area remote. A general view is taken from an indeterminate height. From this vantage you might be on elevated ground, or hovering somewhere above, like the most general spirit of the most general place. Before the aeroplane, an angel or a presiding light, a sign or omen in the sky. Now, more like, a drone. A drone, much like an angel, has eye and agency but, unlike an angel, is void of spirit. A general view is designed not to tell you much. It is bland. There will be nothing to jump out or frighten. Nothing to pin down a mood. There are exceptions to this:

A general view of Dresden, May 1945

The sea photographs well, you could say that. The horizon lines up nice. Waves surge and swell. They roll, they smash, they break . . . all the emotive words. It's just the sea doing its thing. The sea is the most general view of all. From a photograph you might guess at the Atlantic from its colour, size of waves or quality of light, but a horizon at sea is known to be inscrutable.

All her life, the artist Susan Hiller collected postcards. She knew what she was looking for. Rough seas. Views of the sea, or more precisely, vintage views of storms at sea, where giant waves attacked the shore as if to hammer it. The postcards came from a time when people stopped being content with looking and wanted to send pictures of what they saw – or wished to have seen – to one another. Waves storm bulwarks, dwarf piers and drown men. *Something to write home about.* Hiller, an American, chose to come and live on an island. An island is always under attack from outside forces. Sea devours land. Land holds against sea. For the inhabitants of the edge, it is a constant drama.

The postcards came in black and white or sepia, blanched or browned, with additional colour added in by hand as subtle or not-so-subtle tints and washes by studio colourists, most of whom were women, and most of them, uncredited. *Yellow sand. Blue sky.* These were unsung, backroom artists, working in a low-level artform that was fast becoming popular. Postcards were cheap, and readily available. It was boom time for travel and for photography. The faraway was coming near at speed.

Dedicated to the Unknown Artists was the first work she made from this collection, arranging 305 postcards, each titled *Rough Seas*, along with sea charts, map, one book, one dossier, mounted across a set of fourteen, blonde-wood panel frames. A map of the British Isles, annotated according to location, date and written message, is prominent in the first panel, summoning up in compressed form the native obsessions of an island nation; the weather, the seaside, and the vulnerability of its national borders to attack, as a collective imaginary. These are atavistic forces. We are not free of them. The work's subheading is more distanced: *A circumnavigation of the United Kingdom coast arranged according to inshore waters areas.*

Hiller picked up her first *Rough Seas* postcard in Weston-super-Mare. Over and over, in configurations made through her career, she returned to these small images of sea, assembling them in works of disparate geographies and dispositions, large and small, enhanced, reprinted, digitally enlarged and colour washed, mostly arranged in grids or groups under the same generic title. *Rough Seas.*

A grid is a dry choice. A grid jams concepts that might seem worlds apart into one frame, setting them side by side against each other. The sea that hits land at Cromer is the same sea at Clacton and same again at Clevedon. A grid suggests structure, the hope that, under organisation, even the elemental can be brought to heel and marshalled within a single scheme. Hiller's methods were minimal, but the power of the *Rough Seas* postcards and all its variants is maximal. The images are preternaturally stormy. This is the sea as melodrama. The ungovernable is governed. The invisible is made visible. Sublime segues into system. Danger is compacted and so is fear. They're seaside postcards, set disarmingly in rows. We know these places well. On sunny days we stroll along the front with ices.

Seeing the work across a large, white space, the island is small, the postcards puny, the lighting bright and unforgiving. You move in for a closer look. *Ventnor. Whitby. Walton-on-the-Naze.* It is a house of cards. At the level of a single image, 6 × 4, all is agitation. Promenades submerge. Parades turn into flumes. White water becomes wall. Peril is upon the kingdom.

Dedicated to the Unknown Artists was made in the 1970s. Serial, dead-pan and open-ended, it hasn't aged, and slowly, viewed from a distance, a longer form emerges, as can happen with artworks returned to over time, a thickening of meaning, a shift in context, the slow unpacking of a reminder, if you still needed one, that the sea operates in cosmic-historic time and those who live against its borders feel it first, but first or last, we all will feel it.

There is a concrete hut on the South Pier at Newlyn. It's red and white, just like a flag. This is the former Tidal Observatory, where for six years from 1915, observations of water level were taken twenty-four hours a day at fifteen-minute intervals. From this data, Ordnance Datum Newlyn, they set the mean sea level, a benchmark still in use on Ordnance Survey maps as the base from which all elevations across the mainland derive. Our tidal markers are unassuming. The hut is shut. The pier is closed to visitors. The level marked by a bolt embedded in the wall. *You are here.* All heights – above/below – are reckoned from this point.

The sea is rising and as it rises it takes back land. Hall-sands, Foulness, Orwithfleet, Sand le Mere, Waxham Parva, Ravenser Odd . . . the list of ancient villages lost to a collapsing shoreline reads like a poem in a forgotten tongue. The list of towns at risk lined up to join them, in not so many years from now, subject to current rates of rise, storm surge, projected flood trajectory, is readily available to those who care to look online. This time the names are more familiar. Some will be places we ourselves call home: Arbroath and Arundel, Beauly and Blakeney, Camber and Canvey Island . . . just a sample, A to C to test the waters. *I saw this and thought of you.*

Garland was always into maps. He studies them and traces them, draws them in part from memory. I hide my global ignorance carefully from his knowledge. At school, when they were asked to pick a country as a topic, he chose Peru, and spent the maximum of the short time allotted to the project on the cover image, being a map of its area and major landforms. In his rendition there were four main features, the coast being one, and then three others, Lima, the Andes, and Lake Titicaca. The edge took most of his attention. The rest was blank. He took little interest in the borders with its colossal neighbours, and drew a land pressed hard against a sea of its own invention, a coast that stretched 1,500 miles, lovingly shaded down one strip in a sweet fringe of pure, Pacific, coloured-pencil blue.

Maps do not do justice to coasts. On a map, the land gets all the attention – *Of course*, you say, *that's how it is.* Land is a mass of information – an overload of towns and highways, mountains, lakes and colour-coded forests, sites of historic interest and Areas of Outstanding Natural Beauty. The sea is blank. A plain and uneventful blue. To look at maps, you'd think the sea had been deleted. It's out of bounds. Information about the sea is reserved for those who sail on it and those who don't, have little need for guidance. The ocean is unseen for purposes of land . . . therefore it's hard to see. Who learns the history of the deep at school? Its laws? Or its geography? The map shows land and not-land. The one thing, the other thing. It's crude. On a map, the coast is relegated to the edge, giving the land priority, and the sea – Pantone 17-5513 TCX – designates its absence.

A coast is a line on a map, but coasts are whips, not lines, and violence does not sit with being neatly coloured in. I couldn't have named it as a thought myself back then, but age eighteen, I felt the impact of it. Whatever theories I had about the known world, they were narrow. They needed widening. To ready myself in preparation for the widening that I believed was mine to come, I spent a summer working in a harbour town with a mutable population of sailors, tourists, and seasonal workers. It was a place of transience, a portal on the way to somewhere, namely, *North.* A gateway as the Tourist Board would have it. People left all the time; south for work in the cities, and north to experience for a while a kind of isolation not found elsewhere – or simply to disappear. Vast tracts of the North were empty and remain so. Incomers came in to replace those who had left, and for a short time, I was one of them, taking a job as a waitress in one of the many medium-range hotels, an outlier past its middling prime, that lay on the curve of the bay at the point where the town itself ran out, the empty beaches began and continued in the same vein uninterrupted for miles. You could drive that road for hours before arriving somewhere else.

It was a town screwed tight against its presiding water. The harbour was held in common. Engine and pump, clogged at all hours with fishing boats and their expanded kit; dinghies and skiffs, lobster pots, boxes and nets hung on rails, with ferries to and from the islands squeezing expertly and improbably between. I had never been to Alaska – *I had never been anywhere* – but had an idea of it in my head and thought the place might be something like Alaska, beautiful in the right kind of light, but hard to stay in and hard to make a living. The constant transit gave the town an undertow of friction, like the current or drag beneath the surface of a stream that looks innocuous enough but when you dipped your hand in, you felt the cold, and felt too the sharpness of its pull as an intensity, a force that could take you with it.

The harbour was where all the action happened. Leaving and coming back, supplying, refuelling, full nets, empty nets, fighting and fucking, drinking and dancing, drowning, and being saved. Three churches faced each other off the bay. Ten more around the town. The distance from the nightclub at the harbour mouth and the jetty's edge was only a few uncertain metres in the dark. Risky at 4 a.m.

The sea ruled the town with force that bent it into different shapes at will. It was implacable. A group of us would meet at midnight on the harbour wall with beer: the girl from the bar, the chef, the Catalan, the actor, the southern boy on his way north. It was a bond of convenience, formed on the evening shift. We pledged undying friendship, but we were young and all in our own way, passing through. After that summer, we never met again. It was a sea without depth, a sheet of black glass that gouged the town a mouth, ate up its light and bled into all adjoining pools of darkness. We talked the night away, and drank it in.

To give the sea its due, a map should be redrawn in homage to its margins, twinning each coastal town with its own mass in water and including within its boundary, a corresponding area of sea. Then, the all-important shore would not be relegated to the edge, but figure as a live thing, an ever-shifting centre around which the proportions of a town would wrestle from day to night. In flit, grey, light, it was an even match. By night, the balance shifted. By night, the town appeared to shrink, and the sea, vast beyond the defensive lines of boats, swept in. By night, a sea's darkness could suck the wicks from the candles and drag the children from their beds. There is no end to what the sea takes. Maps are silent on our dramas.

Garland is standing on a rock in the sea with Ellen and the other children. From where we sit, it is a general view. The sun is shining. The sea bright greeny-blue. They look so small. I wonder if he is in danger but am too far away to reach him should it occur. I sit with Marsha on a ledge. From here the path is slippery, hard to pick out. It's rocks all the way. How did they get there so quickly anyway? Waves lick the rock in lazy mode, as if the sea is merely flexing before it takes the children down.

You'd think that when your child might be in danger your brain would fire on instinct, spring to their defence, but in fact we watch like passers-by, not quite believing such a scene, a lively sea with its pretty cream fringe, could be anything other than benign.

Where do you think the sea gets its colour?
From its unspeakable, icy depths.

Finally, and much too late, we both stand up embarrassed, like minor characters in a play stumbling on stage. That must have been the reason why we weren't already rushing to retrieve our children. By this time, they are fine. Someone else is leading them off the rock to safety. We hear them laughing far below.

Between stupidity and relief, stupidity has the upper hand and stays that way for a while. Later I imagine the same scene again without the danger. Fear sits so close to love. I am angry, obscurely with him. The sun is still solid gold.

Susan Hiller
Detail from *On the Edge* (2015)
Rough Sea postcards, map,
     482 views of 219 locations,
     mounted on 15 panels
15 frames each: 77.5 × 107.3 ×
     3.2 cm
15 frames each: 30 ½ × 24 ¼ ×
     1 ¼ in

20

Unlike other animals, we make narratives. Turn past experience into new forms and by these forms, we hope, signal to the future. We are alone in this. Here is one, from a sailor's mouth in 1794, on the hounding of the great auk from the last outposts of its terrain:

If you come for their Feathers you do not give yourself the trouble of killing them, but lay hold of one and pluck the best of the Feathers. You then turn the poor Penguin adrift, with his skin half naked and torn off, to perish at his leasure. This is not a very humane method but it is the common practize . . . you burn them alive also to cook their Bodies with. You take a kettle with you into which you put a Penguin or two, you kindle a fire under it, and this fire is absolutely made of the unfortunate Penguins themselves. Their bodys being oily soon produce a Flame; there is no wood on the island.

It was good meat and there was plenty of it. The smell of burnt feathers caught in the sailors' hair and lingered in the clothes they wore for months on end, and under their nails, curls of black wax seasoned the food they ate. We all know how the story goes. The eggs went to collectors, the oil to lamps and the downy feathers into mattresses, hundreds of birds to every one. They made good money.

The island, being rocky and with a sloping shoreline that gave access to abundant fish stocks, was one of the last sites where the great auk could thrive. Island birds in isolation, with no experience of humans have little reason to fear them. The auks were flightless, fluent in water and graceless on land. They did not flee but walked away bemused from their attackers, who came mob-handed to stuff them into canvas bags or herd them up the gangplanks of their boats. Not hunted, they said, but harvested.

A storm is on its way. We stay inside and watch TV. It's *Planet Earth*. Quiet as a man in church, Attenborough is on Ascension, narrating a lone, white fairy tern. On an island with so few predators, the tern doesn't bother with nests. A bare branch is enough. But the egg is broken. The bird paddles in the yolk of her own dead. *She knows something is wrong but her drive to incubate is strong.* He knows what she knows, and now we know it too. Something is wrong. The bird turns her head to camera. Her eyes are black as thousand-year-old coal.

We decide, for purposes of our research, to brave the storm, summon the great auk and go to the spot where it was last recorded. There is no photograph. The creature is lost to us, an illustration drawn from the notes of sailors, eyewitness accounts, or reimagined from stuffed birds in a museum. *Great auk. Alca impennis. Accession number: NHMUK B.277a/1988.21.13.*

In the long afterlife that follows extinction – an unsettling aspect of the Anthropocene – the dodo, another island bird which met a similar fate, fared worse. A dodo in a museum is an artefact, a composite of parts. It's guesswork, glue and wire and chicken feathers. A lone head here, a leg there, a beak, a foot salvaged from storage somewhere else. The dodo as artificially encountered, is an exquisite corpse.

Auks were social and monogamous birds. They mated for life in pairs and cared for their lone young, at the rate of one egg per year, precariously on open ground. From a population of many millions once scattered on islands around the rim of the North Atlantic – St Kilda, Funk Island off Newfoundland, Fowl Craig on Papa Westray, Geirfuglasker, the Great Auk Rock (an old volcanic stub off Iceland) – seventy-eight skins remain on public view.

We designate a spot, a promontory of no distinction at the edge of nowhere we might conceivably find again, stand together, tilt our noses to the sea and pin our anoraks – North Face, taped seams, black and white trim – tight against our sides. In revenge, the wind tears off our hoods and spits us backward onto rock.

21

Everything happens in some place. That's what the ferryman had said when we arrived and in that moment I hadn't understood, but maybe now, after some time, I do, and here, especially here, on such an island, it seems the things that happen can be minute, so small as to be unnoticeable in themselves, so it can seem on the surface as if nothing at all is happening and time passing is rendered as a certain spaciousness or lightness. And taken together, the things that happen coalesce and teem elsewhere, like a school of capelin on open sea, the capelin that in turn will fatten up the cod and take them one year from meagre pickings, to gorged with food the next. And if you wait, everything is visible a season on. Nature rolls over. That is the real mystery. We are forever in arrears.

There is a sea pool in a basin shielded from waves by a natural rim of stone. From Whale Point Bay it is an hour's walk. I'm out of filters, so coffee is a brown sludge in a brown jug but serves to get us going. Garland doesn't need caffeine. Garland has only to open his eyes to be intoxicated. Garland gets going from the moment he wakes, as if the action of waking allows all the drugs of the world at large, of sky and water, air and light to infuse his brain directly via the optic nerve. It is all data, all day long. Garland is therefore busy. He has much to process and by day's end, we're usually exhausted.

To get to the pool you take the path the whole way up the hill then down again to the opposite shore. You can't go round. There is no track, no other way to reach it, no nearby habitations requiring roads to get to them. The Atlantic on this side, most sides, of the island, is not for swimming but for drowning. It's just too wild. Too treacherous. A single wave could tear a person from their mooring and cold would finish them off in a minute. An island is a hindrance in the way of the sea. An obstacle. If it could take it down, it would.

On the eastern shore there is a beach where the flat creek offloads itself into the water. It is more spill than stream and cold as ice. Icebergs passed by not long ago. The rock pares back, slips down and curls to make a secluded level shelf to grant the sea an entry, slow and friendly. The strip of sand it leaves is unexpected. It's the only beach. Water here has travelled a long way. The water's old and cold, and the hit when Garland first jumps in, lights up his face and opens his mouth in shock.

You should try iceberg ice! they said. Ordinary ice, $3.99 a bag. Iceberg ice, $5.99. We are surprised. This is water that's never touched the ground. Antique in origin, split from glaciers off the coast of Greenland, drawn past Newfoundland by the powerful fast-moving current. We would have paid much more.

*

In 1940 Elizabeth Bishop wrote to her friend, the poet Marianne Moore. Words, she said, were *'things' in the head, like icebergs or rocks or awkwardly placed pieces of furniture*. Words were objects to be navigated. They got in the way. You picked them up and put them down again – or threw them out. To move them around was to try to articulate the space of your existence. Words are material but materiality, as we know, is fluid.

We came too late for icebergs. They passed in a narrow window, May to June. To see an iceberg on its way elsewhere would be a wondrous thing. Liquid as solid. Formal as marble. Palatial as green jade. Vast as a merchant ship. It too can melt. Bishop grew up in part in Nova Scotia. She knew what she was talking about. *A thing in the head*. It's a hard thought: could be a threat, a stumbling block, an idea that just won't shift. *How to get round it?*

We drive to Max's Snack Bar, buy a fat chunk of ice in plastic wrap and take it home, but something about its evanescent state unsettles us. We're not sure how to handle it. In the truck, Garland is gentle, cradles it like a cat, but once at home we clear the freezer, shove it in and jam the door shut quick as if to trap it. An iceberg in the freezer is an object out of circulation. It is an error. The taste is airy, smooth and flat, no peaks or troughs, entirely level. It clinks on glass and melts to nothing on the tongue.

The pool is a bright miracle of rock formed centuries ago. Water comes in through a low channel and leaves unseen to create an internal two-way surge, like a hypnotic pulse somewhere within its chamber. The water inside the pool and the water outside are the same, although this makes no sense, being the wholesale substitution of one material state for another, a sleight of hand that's hard to read. Outside, the sea presents as single entity: metallic, light-absorbing, oddly mobile. Inside, the water is subdued and supple, iridescent. It is entirely altered, as canvas might in a particular suspension turn to silk. The water is not warm but nearly, and super-clear as if discreetly lit to make everything at the bottom evenly visible and magnified by the same amount. The rock is richly patterned, like many types of marble poured as liquid and left to settle. Light flicked outwards, always on the edge of vision, as darts, as points, as curves, as curlicues. Black-orange urchins thrived in the shallow tidal space and seaweed in shades of antique bronze hung in the water. Barnacles crowded all the surface rock.

A barnacle has three phases. The first free-floating, feeds on plankton; the second drifting adolescence; and last, a fixed, suspension-feeding adult phase. Its role in the second stage is simply to find a place to live. Once anchored, it will not move again. Garland rejects the urchins near his body, preferring to poke them from above with sticks, but I climb down into the water. I float. I do not flicker. I am the wrong size for flicker-ing. I am the wrong size. Of all the creatures here assembled, visible and invisible, I have been gifted the least grace. I fill the pool, displace the water, blot the sun. The waves beyond the rocks are a distant force. It is calm. Above me, there is only sky.

I did not always trust in water. Once I could no more swim across a pool than levitate its length by thought alone. As a child I was afraid. My fingers held to the edge and my feet clung in the shallows. To swim was to anticipate panic, there-fore I didn't swim. The act of swimming, like riding a bicycle, is an embodied pleasure, automatic, useful but not consid-ered valuable enough to be of note. Anyone can learn to swim, they say, or drive, or ride a bike. To acquire the skill is simply to move into the ranks of those who can, as opposed to those who can't. It is a manual shift, procedural, a simple crossing from one state into another. The leap of faith, the fear, and all that went before is quickly forgotten in the sheer joy of forward motion. Once on the other side, you don't look back.

There is a photograph from Jo Spence's series *The Final Project* (1991–92) in which Spence floats in water over a bare field. She looks at home. It was the floating, the ease of it, that caught my attention first and only then the field, so nondescript, it could be any field, but seemed somehow familiar. I thought I recognised it. For a while we lived beside a landscape much like this, of cabbage fields receding hand in hand in rows, stuck with the odd hamlet and overlaid with the background hum of the A2 at a level so low and constant you might think it existed only in your head. It was a stagnant prospect, formed between the tidal pull of London and the outflow of the Thames. I never learned to love it.

It is a strange, affecting image, made from two photos jammed together, both in themselves quite plain. Montage was Spence's mode in later years, the putting of images together, she called it *slide sandwiching*. Before computers, it was as simple as layering two slides, like cheese on ham, and printing them. That's often how you make new things. Stick them together. One on another. Presence and absence; weightlessness and gravity; prosaic and visionary; life and death.

Spence wears a black swimsuit. She is absorbed. You might have seen her on a quiet Tuesday in the swimming pool of any recreation centre, arms out, body in float, in thrall to no one's schedule but her own. I've been there many times: weightless, ears stopped by water, eyes adjusting to the light, my breathing slowed, holding gravity at bay a while, keeping time and all the other things that time will make us answer to at bay for just a little longer. By the time she made the image, Spence knew she was dying. Exhausted by illness, she could no longer take new pictures but turned to pre-existing works, repurposing her own image over and over for her own ends. Sticking herself then on to herself now. Sending herself into the future. *How do you make leukaemia visible?* she asked. *Well, how do you? It's an impossibility.*

She is an English effigy: a middle-aged mystic in a one-piece. Her hands are open and outstretched. Surrender, supplication, acceptance, thanksgiving after rain. It is a gesture of multiple compliances, not of mourning. Looking for ripples in the water amidst the blue, you see the patterns are not waves but marks of tyres. The swerve of a tractor at the end of a long furrow echoes a clumsy tumble, or the mistimed turn of a lane swimmer. She is both land and water. Earth goes under her. Water around her. Tyre tracks mark her down.

Spence was not known for peaceful images. The opposite in fact. The camera was a weapon. She was a sniper. She had her targets well within her sights. *Jo Spence, Photographer: Available for Divorces, Funerals, Illness, Social Injustice, Scenes of Domestic Violence, Explorations of Sexuality and any Joyful Events.* Her images are angry, fearless, funny. Often she jokes around. Death was the final project and like her other projects, faced head on. Once seen, her photos tend to stick.

The piece was one of a series made with Terry Dennett, her long-time collaborator. It is a monument of sorts. The earth beneath does not bury her but lifts her. Holds her gently in the image forever. This is what a photograph can do. Hold a person in an image forever. And contrary to what you might expect, a photo doesn't fix a person down, but over time releases them. It is a slow release, diffuse and gentle. The context fades, the photo slips. The death happened. The image remains. A person can float free.

Jo Spence
The Final Project: (End Picture, Floating), 1991–92
Positive print from medium-format colour negative
89 × 134 cm
Collaboration with Terry Dennett

22

I'm in a shower. It's nothing really. Basic. No epiphany. A hand shower has been rigged on to a hook outside to spurt out a circle of warmish water at a difficult angle. I can't skew my body under the spray, and I can't train the spray onto my head because the hook won't move. It's fixed. It's an open-roofed shower, essentially a wooden box, set up outside the house of friends who live along the southern shore beside a little patch of wood that stops abruptly where it meets the sea.

A blood-warm, slow dissolving rain is falling. Under the shower, the rain is not apparent. Against a sky of the exact same shade as rain, you just can't see it, so you wouldn't know. It's very early; daylight barely there. We came for drinks and it got late. We stayed the night and here I am alone, just me, awake. As rain hits the box enclosure to meet the rising warmth of the shower, a light steam forms to blur the lines of the box, the edge and the upward view of a sky that is already blurred. Definition is low. It's an eighteen per cent grey.

The shower is a cubicle, more an upright crate. It can accommodate a single person standing but not by much. I hold myself centred in the space, skin on alert for splinters. It's crude, but there is something about the shape, the top open to the sky and the average-person size of it that matches me and suits the hour. It's like a private sky-space, custom-built, that sets me outside the waking world in my container and brings the sky's column down to where I stand, to make a single, solitary, skyward-looking eye. There's nothing to see. Rain falls as drops on my lens.

The air inside is warm. The box cuts out the wind. Standing in a wooden box, upright, and not a coffin, I have a patch of time cut to a rough shape that roughly fits. Slowly the time expands to fill. I watch the dirt that rims my feet wash out into the basin and disappear.

The square of sky is pearl and thick as felt soaked overnight in water but unlike felt, it's luminous, backed by the covert sun. Millions of miles of old and unrecorded light narrow to this point in time. It is unreadable. Unseeable. Water and light at full chromatic stretch. The sky is a wet weight. If it could fall, that sky would suffocate me in an instant. Stop my mouth forever.

I try to gauge the point where rain first forms. How far can the eye go in the mass? Drops don't fall in lines or rods but whirl and float in an uncertain blizzard, more like snow than rain. It is haphazard. Rain is on me before I see it. Everything is on me before I see it. The ratio of me to sky is small. The sky has me naked in its sights but I have a single square of it to view. There's something else – *What is that?* – something above the noise of water. A sound . . . an unintelligible sound. Somewhere beyond the frame there is a bird. I do not know its song. The bird has the advantage. It has the axis of the sky while I am fixed within a shape that measures five by five. The fitful shower has galvanised, it's suddenly in spate. A stream of notes is falling in the water.

A mote or speck of grey, floats against its own background. At such long range, there's little to differentiate something – a bird, say – from its native air. It could be a plastic bag caught on the current, a balloon, a drone, a dust-spot, a spider web in my eye – or nothing. But the ear has it. The ear has it sharp as a drill in diamond action, with a refrain we cannot hope to emulate. It is the speech-song of an outsider making its mark. A vertical verse that falls. Cadence. Chorus. Pause. Repeat.

Someone is rattling the latch. It must be time. An engine starts up elsewhere as if in another life. Time is the thing I want. Time. *Where has the time gone?* My clothes. *Where are my clothes?* Ingenuity has not been tested here. There is no peg. No peg means nowhere to hang your clothes. The towel is wet.

The sound is muddy now. The song drains out like liquid and with it, all iridescence fades as suddenly as it appeared. Without that voice, re-amplified within its frame, the sky goes quiet. It seals to make a lid. Garland's voice signals the day's emergence, the slow round-up of people, clothes, and goods. The door swings on the latch. We're going home.

This is the *last times* week. The last time to the beach to swim. Last time we get to drive the truck. Last time we see our friends in town. Last time at the ice-cream store. This week we make a circuit of all the last times things and cross them off each one. We count the days till our departure, soon it will be the hours. The act of counting won't make leaving easier but gives it frame. *How to take leave of landscape?* Same way as meeting it. By walking. Today we walk the high ground behind the house but this time it will be different. This is the last time.

The hill behind the house is steep and we think to go as far as the ridge we've walked so many times before. Low on the trail, past the bush we now know to be full of hornets and the tree blasted by wind to necromantic shapes, we meet a man in better walking gear than ours. He is a geologist, one of many drawn to the island by the live record enacted in its rocks. We saw them everywhere. Sometimes they walked alone, as if tuned in to private, listening mode, or fanned in clusters across the landscape, attending to the rock as if it were a living thing as was its due, drawing attention back from the all-consuming sky and down to earth. Granite vs gabbro. The land that was liquid.

Time is on the side of geologists. They do not need to hurry. Scanning the ground, he reads its composition like chapters in a textbook over a long span. Hiking the trails for him is fieldwork and his canvas bag is ever ready for finds. For company, he walks us part-way up the ridge. We fall in step.

Glacial erratics is his subject. These are the ice-borne rock anomalies, the lonely ones, he says, like charismatic preachers still shouting of landscapes far away and long ago. He points out a rock that stands out sharp against the sky in isolation. *Of course!* We nod. Once seen, it seems so obvious an interloper, clearly a teleport in space and time, a foreigner. We bring our hands together for a moment on its mass, palms flat, as if to get its measure. Quartz sparks where the light hits and it is warm, but just as quickly when we turn to leave, I'm not so sure I pick it out again along the crowded ridge. It's a plutonic landscape: the ground beneath our feet is everywhere arrested, caught mid-flow, the colours from an arcane register of oxblood, garnet and stone-cold, long-dead furnace. He waves his arms across the scene as if to call the stones upstanding to our attention. *The full spectrum of the magma chamber . . .* It's rocks as far as the eye can see.

There is a photograph by Diane Arbus, *Rocks on Wheels*. The title has it down. A group of fake rocks are marshalled as if in a siding, ready to pass as landscape in a desert setting. It is a small, uncommon image that speaks to another time and place. Of all her pictures, it has stayed with me. Arbus didn't much go in for landscapes. This one is rare and very early, before she worked out who her subjects were and set them up within her sights to shoot. It looks like dawn. The world is coming into being. Rocks wait in the wings. The workers who must push the boulders forward on their dollies haven't yet clocked in. The landscape is arid, rocky. *Why would it need more rocks?* The print is titled, rear, top left, in pencil: *Rocks on Wheels*, Disneyland, California, 1963.

Wind, rock, horizon – all conspire to keep the centre of gravity low. The ground would have taken all our attention had not the sky been so dominant from edge to edge. The light that morning sent the camera mad. When you take a photograph of the skies of the North, the great chasing skies, the lens sometimes doesn't cope and bursts the tones wide open, so they look more extreme than they are in life. The cloud whites are smeared in all colours and the cloud yolks, dirty yellow. The greys are so diverse they make a separate chart in themselves that runs from *Asphalt* up to and including *Zinc*. Every colour will have its roots in every other shade, mixed up at source. The grey has yellow and also black. The black has pink folded inside. But no one ever calls the sky a mess though, do they? Or crude. They just accept it. We just accepted it. The sky was a cathedral erected daily in place.

These were the high points, steep but navigable. Birch came in two sizes, small and smaller. There was swamp birch that hugged the rock and stunted birch to the knee. There were few trees, mainly spruce or fir and skinny, big on wind resistance but didn't get much height. Wind scraped the hill bare in all directions. Salt did the rest. The ground was creeping juniper and common juniper, those were the ones I knew, and bearberry and partridgeberry – the one that's called the lingon – with honeysuckle chasing through to muddle them. Should all the berries come out at once, the earth would blacken with their juice but now was not their time – two weeks, or maybe three – after we'd gone – to ripen. Pitcher plants the colour of old blood lined the upper marshes and Garland sought them out to watch flies drown in their mouths. Fragile sundews drank the air. Horsetail, the prehistoric one, seeded itself in hollows, and on the island's eastern side, waves of imperial iris grew.

Shut your eyes and you could hear the ground as much as see it. Leaves were crisp and tough, not tender. Sharp, sun-baked, salt-hardened, full of fire. Tender is not an island's nature. The visible set the stage for the audible in a fiery crack of rock-based, rolling bloom. Plants dug their roots into the soil to fractions of a millimetre, grasping for purchase in crevices and cracks and coating the rock in a tenacious mat of small and ever smaller plants, riven with bugs and insects, hauling the debris of their lives along the while and when it was over, leaving their bodies as depositions on the same ground for us to walk on. Lichen, the polymorph, was everywhere – like leaf, like lace, like moss, like paint . . .

so prolific it came with its own guidebook. Lichen was the backdrop on which all other plants were painted.

Paths were few. Out on the hill you made your own track and the land responded accordingly. Each step was an event, a quake that compressed the cosmos skin-thin into the fragile soil. We picked our way with care. A single footfall might crush a thousand living things but cause another thousand to bounce back the stronger. Broken stems held seams of hidden moisture. Pods detonated into seed as Garland jumped on them. He stopped to set one stone upon another to make a cairn. Leaving his mark. We passed this way.

When he was four years old, Garland passed through a stage of drawing landscape as flat zones separate from one other. The ground was a felt-tipped bar that hugged the bottom of the page and the sky a blue strip along the top, with an expanse of A4 paper, containing the sun untethered to either sphere, sandwiched between. Now he would see it differently. Sketch out the path, outline the hilltop carefully in pen, press harder on the rocks in shade to darken them, but there was something true and elementary about this depiction. That was where we were, out in the middle section, empty and blank. We were a small party. Three. Two. One. From here, the land lay flat for our inspection. We climbed together, walking the narrow gradient between sky and ground.

The geologist says he doesn't know when the rain will come. I don't know why I asked him, confusing perhaps geology with meteorology as if knowledge of rocks and their kinetic gifts has made him a master of prediction. He answers out of politeness, but his guess is as good as mine. Clouds on the hill are massing. It's time to leave. We say our goodbyes and press ahead.

Rain hits within ten minutes on the trail. Lichens swell. Pines take in water. The granite blots to ever darker pink. Alpines and low-growing shrubs mark the subarctic fauna and as we climb, the plants get shorter, as if in climbing you truly leave all height behind and move towards a final, scoured flatness where nothing withstands the wind, and the ultimate surface texture is velvet.

Notes & credits

p. 25,   'Lesson 1 . . .': *First Lessons in Geography*, from James Monteith's Geographical Series (A. S. Barnes and Company, 1884)

p. 33,   Felix Gonzalez-Torres
"Untitled", 1991
Print on paper, endless copies
© Estate Felix Gonzalez-Torres
Courtesy of The Felix Gonzalez-Torres Foundation

p. 35,   'Ross. The public was Ross . . .': 'Feliz Gonzalez-Torres: Être un espion', interview with Felix Gonzalez-Torres by Robert Storr, ArtPress (Paris), January 1995, https://creativetime.org/programs/archive/2000/Torres/torres/storr.html

p. 43,   'Oh Captain tell me true . . .': 'What Did the Deep Sea Say?', trad., arranged by Woody Guthrie

p. 46,   'There are three types . . .': National Oceanic and Atmospheric Administration, https://oceanexplorer.noaa.gov/facats/plate-boundaries.html#~:text=There%20are%20three%20kinds%20of%20%20the%20U.S.%20Geological%20Survey

p. 76,   'Deposition occurs . . .': https://geoteach2017.weebly.com/coastal-processes.html

p. 79,   'Staring, open-mouth face . . .': https://nationalzoo.si.edu/animals/ring-tailed-lemur

p. 89,   Rose Finn-Kelcey
The Restless Image: a discrepancy between the seen position and the felt position, 1975
© The Estate of Rose Finn-Kelcey and Kate MacGarry

p. 133,   'It's such a nice symmetrical ocean . . .': www.nytimes.com/2006/08/26/obituaries/26tharp.html

p. 145, 'What is an Island? . . .': *First Lessons in Geography*, from James Monteith's Geographical Series (1884, A. S. Barnes and Company)

p. 146, 'What is an Ocean? . . .': ibid.

p. 173, Susan Hiller
Detail from *On the Edge*, 2015
Rough Sea postcards, map, 482 views of 219 locations, mounted on 15 panels
© The Estate of Susan Hiller
Courtesy of Lisson Gallery

p. 187, 'If you come for their Feathers . . .': from the account of Aaron Thomas, an English seaman who sailed to Newfoundland on HMS *Boston*, www.audobon.org/news /excerpt-sixth-extinction-unnatural-history

p. 191, Jo Spence
The Final Project: (End Picture, Floating), 1991–92
© Estate of Jo Spence
Courtesy of Richard Saltoun Gallery, London, Rome and New York

p. 195, '"things" in the head . . .': Elizabeth Bishop to Marianne Moore, 11 September 1940, Elizabeth Bishop, *One Art: The Selected Letters*, ed. Robert Giroux (Pimlico, 1994)

p. 198, 'How do you make leukaemia visible? . . .': Jo Spence, *The Final Project* (Ridinghouse Editions, 2013)

p. 198, 'Jo Spence, Photographer . . .': from the business card of Jo Spence; Jo Spence, *Putting Myself in the Picture: A Political, Personal and Photographic Autobiography* (Camden Press, 1986)

All other images © Marion Coutts, Fogo Island/ The Change Islands

Acknowledgements

This book was not written at speed. It came together slowly over time in different places with the support of the following institutions. I would like to thank them.

Fogo Island Arts, which hosted us, in association with Art Metropole, through the Islands Arts Writing Residency, on Fogo Island, Newfoundland, and Artscape, Toronto Island.

Cove Park residency programme, Argyll, Scotland.

A visiting research fellowship at the Henry Moore Institute in Leeds.

The art department at Goldsmiths, University of London, which provided research leave at a key moment.

The names of places and people have been changed, with the exception of artists, whose work is clearly identifiable. I am very grateful to the estates of Felix Gonzalez-Torres, Rose Finn-Kelcey, Susan Hiller and Jo Spence for permission to reproduce their work. These are artists I have long admired. The photos of the sea and coastal rock formations were taken on Fogo Island. 'What Did the Deep Sea Say?' is the title of a traditional song I first heard in a version by Woody Guthrie.

Many friends and supporters were crucial to the development of this book. Huge thanks to them.

Sharon Topper and Zoe Lewis in Provincetown, who took us in when we most needed it.

Jenny Turner, my first reader.

Michal Shavit, Seán Hayes and David Milner, my editors at Fern Press and VINTAGE, and the brilliant team there who took such care with this publication.

My agent, Anna Webber, at A. M. Heath.

The friends we made on Fogo, for welcoming us and sharing their experience of the island.

Friends and colleagues in London, for their constant encouragement when writing stalled.

My son, Eugene.